Simple
Scrollsaw Projects

Simple
Scrollsaw Projects

GUILD OF MASTER CRAFTSMAN PUBLICATIONS LTD

This collection first published 2000 by
Guild of Master Craftsman Publications Ltd,
Castle Place, 166 High Street, Lewes,
East Sussex BN7 1XU

© GMC Publications 2000

ISBN 1 86108 180 4

A catalogue record of this book is available from the British Library

Front cover photographs, left to right, top to bottom:
Christine Richardson, Christine Richardson, Christine Richardson,
John Everett, Tim Foxall

Back cover photographs:
Christine Richardson

Article photography by the individual project authors

Printed and bound by Kyodo Printing (Singapore) under the
supervision of MRM Graphics, Winslow, Buckinghamshire, UK

Contents

Note

Every effort has been made to ensure that the information in this book is accurate at the time of writing but inevitably prices, specifications, and availability of tools will change from time to time. Readers are therefore urged to contact manufacturers or suppliers for up-to-date information before ordering tools.

Measurements

Throughout the book instances may be found where a metric measurement has fractionally varying imperial equivalents, usually within $\frac{1}{16}$in either way. This is because in each particular case the closest imperial equivalent has been given. A mixture of metric and imperial measurements should never be used – always use either one or the other.

See also detailed metric/imperial conversion charts on page 124.

Introduction

Scrollsawing is one of the fastest growing crafts of modern times. Some of the world's best known exponents of the art reveal their secrets to lead the way forward with new techniques and developments.

All the authors are acknowledged in the world of the scrollsaw for their imagination and expertise, and many are professional craftsmen. The reader, therefore, can be confident that the projects featured throughout are uncluttered by unproven practices and theories, outdated techniques or impractical approaches. All represent a valid source of up-to-the-minute information.

In these pages you will find fresh project ideas, using the wide variety of materials that can be worked with the scrollsaw. An easy to follow step-by-step format ensures success, whatever the skill level of the reader.

Ideas and inspirations from the world of the scrollsaw give the reader the capability to produce unlimited and very beautiful works without the assistance of other machining processes.

Paul Richardson
Managing Editor (Magazines)

Reflected glory

John Everett shows how to make a simple but effective bevel mirror overlay

Materials

- A mirror. The one used here is from the hand-made range of bevelled mirrors from Kaye – D Mirrors and is 225mm (8$\frac{7}{8}$in) diameter. These mirrors are surprisingly inexpensive considering they are hand-made and are of excellent quality. Phone/Fax 01908 612236 for price list/catalogue
- 4 pieces of hardwood, 3–4mm ($\frac{1}{8}$in – $\frac{3}{16}$in) thick and 56mm x 266mm (2$\frac{1}{4}$in x 10$\frac{1}{2}$in) for the front of the mirror
- 2 pieces of hardwood, 3–4mm ($\frac{1}{8}$in – $\frac{3}{16}$in) thick and 92mm x 53mm (3$\frac{5}{8}$in x 2$\frac{1}{8}$in)
- 2 pieces of hardwood, 3–4mm ($\frac{1}{8}$in – $\frac{3}{16}$in) thick and 80mm x 38mm (3$\frac{1}{8}$in x 1$\frac{1}{2}$in)
- 2 pieces of 3–4mm MDF, 245mm (9$\frac{5}{8}$in) square
- Small woodscrews – brass is best to avoid staining – 10mm ($\frac{3}{8}$in) x 4 are good
- Screw eyes and picture wire for hanging the mirror
- A little wood glue and Spraymount glue

With a circular mirror, even a very good one with a bevelled edge such as that used for this project, there can be a problem making a frame or surround for it in that the widths of wood required (if wood is to be used rather than the dreaded MDF), are simply not available, particularly if thin panels are used to avoid that awful 'chunky' look suffered by so many scrollsaw designs. That said, there is of course, a simple answer to the problem. Make the surround in four smaller pieces much as you would if you were constructing a picture frame and mitre the corners. Although the wood used in this project is thin, mostly around 3–4 mm ($\frac{1}{8}$in – $\frac{3}{16}$in) in thickness, once the complete frame has been assembled and glued together, it will be more than adequate in terms of strength for its purpose.

This project suggests a solution to the problem of a mirror surround with mitred corners which not everyone will be able to make meet up precisely along the length of all four mitres. It is a case of – if you

can't hide it, make a feature of it. This is done in this project as can be seen from the pictures, by tracing the outline of actual oak leaves and cutting them from small offcuts of decent hardwood and placing them in opposing pairs over the mitres to complete the design of the front of the mirror surround as well as completely obscuring the actual mitres.

The mirror project is a useful exercise in cutting straight lines, gentle but accurate curves, small, fairly intricate detailing and matching up the rear, unseen parts of the project which consist of the mirror retaining panel and the back plate which secures the mirror into the whole framework. The completed item comprises the four individual front panel pieces with their decorative overlays in the form of oak leaves, the mirror itself, a mirror retaining frame and a back plate. The decoration (the oak leaves) has not been 'overdone' in order to preserve a clean, almost classical design without excessive 'fussy' detail which would spoil the look of the finished item.

Mark up the blanks

Stick down the cutting pattern

external cut on both pieces. Clean off any saw tear out once you have finished cutting with a little fine sandpaper.

1 Mark up the blanks for the two pieces of MDF or ply using the cutting pattern as a guide.

2 Stick down the cutting pattern with spraymount adhesive. You will only need one of the MDF pieces at this point as the internal cutout to accommodate the mirror is made in the top piece only, the remaining piece serves to secure the mirror as a backing sheet. Mark out and drill a starter hole to make the internal circular cutout on the sheet with the cutting pattern.

3 Cut out the circular hole which will accommodate the mirror. You will need to check the dimensions

given against the actual mirror you have as there may well be some slight variation in dimensions of the mirror and you will need to adjust the size of the circular cutout accordingly. The mirror needs to be a fairly snug fit within this cutout, but not too tight to prevent slight expansion and contraction with temperature changes throughout the year.

4 Once you have completed the circular cutout, use the mirror to check for a good fit before proceeding on to the next step.

5 Next make a 'stack' of the two MDF pieces with the cutting pattern on top and cut around the

6 The next step is to make up a stack of the four blanks for the front of the mirror surround with the cutting pattern in place on the top piece. You will need to take care when you cut along the lines which will form the mitres where the four pieces meet in a square. You can of course, adjust these lines after cutting with a sandpaper block but it is always better to cut accurately in the first place. Cut these parts out carefully and clean up after sawing with fine sandpaper.

Cut around the external shape

Cut out the circular hole

Use the mirror to check fit

Make a stack for the front

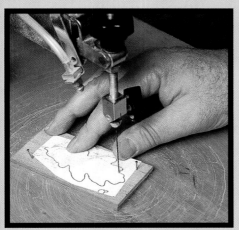

Make up oak leaf blanks in stacks

Apply oak leaf shapes over the mitre corners

7 Make up the two pairs of oak leaf blanks in stacks with their cutting patterns and cut out carefully. Once cut out, you can round off the edges of the 'leaves' if you prefer, or simply leave them square as they came from the saw as was done in the example shown here.

8 Lay out the four parts of the front of the mirror frame and check for accurate fit, particularly at the mitres and inner and outer edges of each piece. Sand to fit as may be necessary. Now run a little wood glue into each mitre and join the pieces on a flat surface. Next apply wood glue to the back of the leaves and place these in position over each mitre joint. On the one

shown, one leaf of each pair was reversed to balance the design. The smaller leaves go to the top of the mirror and the larger ones at the bottom. Add some weight to the frame and leave for the glue to set thoroughly.

9 Once the glue has set, you can glue the mirror retaining frame in place at the back of the main frame. When this glue has set, carry out any decorating or

finishing to the frame as you feel appropriate. The one shown here was given two coats of wax polish front and back and allowed to dry properly before completion. That done, place the mirror in its retaining frame and screw down the backing sheet. Fit the screw eyes and picture wire to hang your mirror.

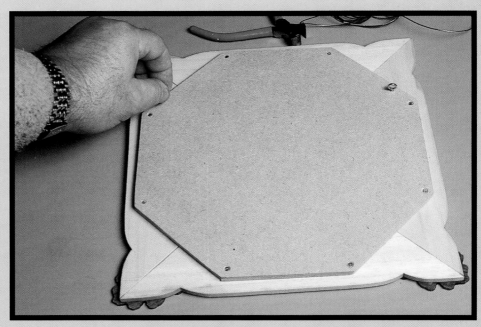

Fix mirror retaining frame in place

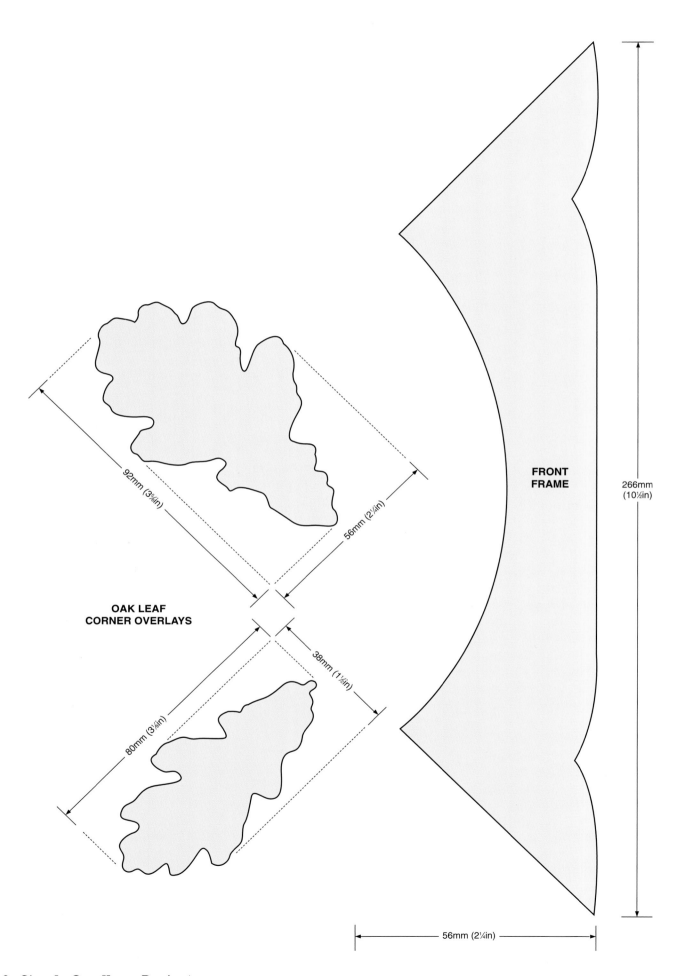

OAK LEAF
CORNER OVERLAYS

92mm (3⅝in)

56mm (2¼in)

80mm (3⅛in)

38mm (1½in)

FRONT
FRAME

266mm
(10½in)

56mm (2¼in)

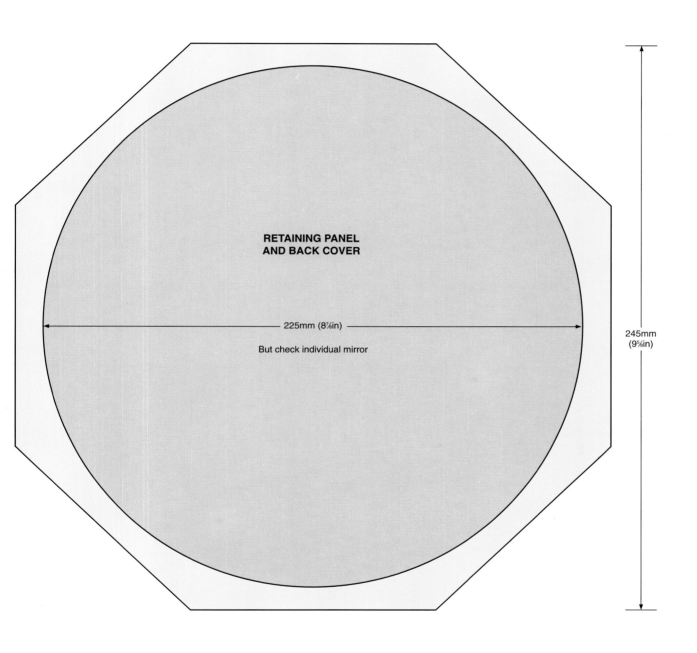

RETAINING PANEL
AND BACK COVER

225mm (8⅞in)

But check individual mirror

245mm
(9⅝in)

Signs of the times

Tim Foxall says that making signs are a directly useful way of using a scrollsaw

Making signs gives you a bit of a buzz, especially seeing your work being given pride of place outside local houses.

I recently read a graphic design book which treated typeface designers as superstars. I thought that this was rather strange until I realised that you invent a typeface, call it some zappy name, and then billions and billions of words are written using it. There is no doubt that there is a place for beautifully precise cut-out lettering, complete with exaggerated serifs (the tops and tails).

However, I have nightmares measuring out all the letters to make them all perfectly uniform with identical stroke widths, angles, frilly bits and tapers. Having cut it all out, I then realise that I had left out a letter.

Bubble alphabet

Most of the signs that I, and students make are derived from a bubble alphabet, with the letters joined together. Although it is a good idea for the letters to have vaguely relative sizes, there is considerable leeway, and you can actually exaggerate parts of some letters, which can sometimes look more convincing than having one letter slightly larger than the rest.

Unless you are going confidently over the top for a design reason, you usually draw horizontal containing lines that you more or less adhere too. There are a number of basic rules to make the bubble signs convincing, and to make sure that they are readable by passing motorists. The main rule is to include the house number, as in many cases they are more important than a name.

Start with capitals

I have started with the capital letters, because they are the easiest to draw out and cut around, although I personally think that signs are more interesting if they feature a mixture of capital letters to start the words and lower case letters for the rest. There are certainly more possibilities to design a more pictorial sign – of that, more later on.

Cutting out

Cutting out the letters and sticking them onto a backing has great benefits. By far the most terrifying commission was to carve complicated lettering on the back of a wonderful bench that someone else had

made, complete with its interlocking curved solid teak tracery. All right, it was a hot day, but the carving was getting soaked with sweat from my forehead, thinking that I would have to replace the whole bench if I made a mistake and carved 'May' instead of 'Mary'.

Recently I have been talking to a stone-carver friend who is halfway through carving 'Highland Distillers' in situ on an immaculate sandstone facing, hopefully on the front of the Highland Distillers building. Having to replace a whole building if you make a mistake - wow!

Unless you are cutting the name out of thick hardwood with bubblier than normal letters, the signs are usually far stronger if they are fixed to a backing, preferably screwed from the back (this is another reason why it is sensible to join up the letters).

You can also separate the two by plywood washers so that rainwater drains off more easily, and to give more of a 3D effect. If it is to go in an exposed location, it is also an option to soak the sign with wood preservative, and to coat it with several layers of exterior varnish or teak oil, although you have the insurance that if a revarnishing/oiling regime is not kept up, it is easy to sand just the face of the sign, and this makes it look even more 3D. It also helps if you use a hardwood like oak that has natural non-rotting agents.

General

The letters are easier to mark out if you draw the complete letters, including the overlaps, and then rub out the extra bits of the lines so that you don't start sawing along them by mistake. Any bits left over at the end can be sanded off (see photographs).

Wherever possible, drill holes for the centre so that:

   a) you don't need to take the blade off
   b) they generally look neater.

It is important to drill the holes before cutting out the sign in case the wood splits.

The join should be a compromise between making the letters individual and still being a strong enough join. In other words, the letter should be seen to be coming to an end, curving inwards.

In general, make the joins between letters sharp and the parts of individual letters rounded.

The Olsen reverse-ground blades are perfect for signs, with the clean edges and minimal break-out.

CAPITALS

Inside has to be sawn ('O' confusion).
Also make angles on left sharp.

Bottom hole larger than top one.

More usually joined at top.

If a choice, join letters at bottom for stable look (like 'E' or 'C').

Bigger than other holes exaggerate base (obviously not a failed perfect circle).

No option but sawing.

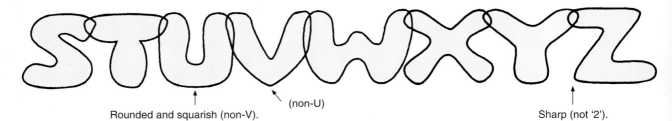

Rounded and squarish (non-V).

(non-U)

Sharp (not '2').

NUMBERS

Again, like the letter 'O', an exaggeratedly large base and off-centre top.

Alternative '4' ➔

Larger base (usually join here).

Make a splash

Especially for the children is this friendly dolphin clock by **John Everett**

As the dolphin is particularly popular with children, it seemed an obvious choice of design for a bedroom or nursery clock. The dolphin design, coupled with a clearly numbered chapter ring and accurate quartz clock movement makes this a suitable project for any child's room. It has the added advantage of encouraging time-telling by other than purely digital means.

The 'dolphin' itself is made from 6mm (¼in) MDF material although there is no reason why other materials such as ply or even a piece of timber could not be used. The actual amount of material needed is small and consists of just one piece of, in this case, some MDF 550mm x 225mm (22in x 11in). If an alternative thickness of material is used, then it may be necessary to order a longer or shorter spindle length for the clock movement. The movement used here is the Super C.I. Imperial Quartz Movement and can be bought in three spindle lengths to accommodate panel thicknesses from 3mm to 16mm (⅛in–⅝in).

The pattern gives the cutting and decorating pattern and has a 25mm (1in) grid to allow it to be copied to the correct size to accommodate a 100mm (4in) chapter ring. A100mm (4in) chapter ring is quite large enough to be read easily but, bearing in mind that a dolphin has a long narrow shape, not so large as to make the dolphin itself too large to be practical. The clock movement itself has a hanger moulded into its casing so the only other item you need is a single-pin picture hanger to mount the finished clock.

1 First, you will need a cutting pattern. This can be either drawn freehand based on the drawing here or photocopied to size direct from the page.

2 Cut around the outline to leave around half an inch excess and mark round the paper pattern with a pencil to make a 'blank' for final cutting. Having cut out your blank which is simple with a jigsaw, although other types of saw will do just as well, lightly sand the edges to remove any debris left from the sawing operation. Next stick your cutting pattern onto the blank. Spraymount adhesive is best if you have it but again, most non-permanent types of paper glue will do the trick.

3 Having stuck the cutting pattern onto your blank, first drill the spindle hole. This needs to be a clearance hole for the brass

▲ **Gluing the cutting pattern onto MDF blank ready for sawing**

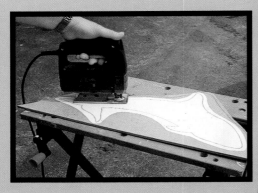

▲ Using a jigsaw with thin blade to cut out the dolphin shape

▲ The cut out and drilled dolphin ready for decoration

locking ring which secures the clock movement in place. This is an 8mm drill in the case of the movement used in the example shown here.

4 The next job is to cut out the dolphin shape. This is not too difficult to do with a narrow blade in a jigsaw but easiest of all in a power fretsaw. Simply follow the outline on the cutting pattern with the saw blade. Once you have completed the cut, sand the edges to leave a smooth surface for decorating the dolphin.

5 The decorating is done next before fitting the chapter ring. First give the dolphin an overall coat of primer/sealer. A white acrylic primer/sealer was used here as it is very quick drying, water based and non-toxic.

6 Next add the colours of your choice or follow the colours used in the picture. If you are not too sure about this stage, then make a light pencil line to indicate where the colours need to be applied as a guide. Once your colours have dried, you can

apply a couple of coats of acrylic varnish to leave a wipe-clean surface.

7 The chapter ring is next. The quickest and easiest method of attaching this is to use a high speed epoxy adhesive. The type used here sets in just four minutes which gives ample time to locate the chapter ring and need only be applied to the chapter ring itself so does not leave any surplus adhesive anywhere it is not wanted. In order to accurately locate the 'twelve o'clock' position, suspend the dolphin by passing the handle of a brush or

round pencil through the spindle hole and let it hang. As this is the position the clock will assume when completed, fitting the chapter ring in this way will ensure that the numerals are correctly located. Mix up a little epoxy resin and smooth it thinly onto the back of the chapter ring. Check the location of the chapter ring relevant to the 'twelve o'clock' position and that it is centred over the spindle hole and lay it in place. A little light pressure to ensure the chapter ring is in place all round and leave for the required five minutes.

▲ The painted dolphin ready for fitting the chapter ring and clock movement

▲ Checking the position of the chapter ring before gluing in position

8 All that remains now is to fit the clock movement and the hands. The clock movement specified is supplied with a rubber washer which fits over the spindle and sits neatly over an extrusion on the moulded casing of the movement. Fit the washer and pass the spindle through the hole in the dolphin. Now spin on the brass locking collar until it is finger tight.

9 Check that the hanger on the rear of the movement is lined up with the 'twelve o'clock' position on the chapter ring and finally tighten the locking collar. This can be achieved with the jaws of a pair of miniature pointed-nose pliers. Insert the plier jaws into the slots either side of the locking collar and carefully rotate the pliers until the collar is tight, making sure the movement does not rotate out of position.

10 Now to fit the hands to the clock. The hands, as supplied with the movement, have a nearly invisible protective plastic covering to prevent them from scratching. Find and remove this thin plastic sheet. Tweezers are a great help in this step. Now take the hour hand and line it up with the 'twelve o'clock' position on the dial and push firmly with a finger with side of the centre bush. The hand will slide fairly easily into position and does not require too much force. Now repeat this procedure for the minute hand. That done, fit the second hand into the hole in the centre of the spindle.

11 Your clock is now complete and requires only the insertion of a battery and setting to the correct time using the little thumb wheel on the rear of the movement.

Suppliers

Clock movement, chapter ring and hands
Yorkshire Clock Builders,
654, Chesterfield Road,
Woodseats,
Sheffield S8 0SB.
Tel. 0114 255 0786
Catalogue available on request.

Epoxy Adhesive
W. Hobby Ltd.,
Knight's Hill Square,
London SE27 0HH.
Tel. 0208 7614244
Catalogue available on request.

MDF 6mm sheet, paint etc.
Any local DIY outlet.

▲ Suspending the dolphin to hang freely to check the 'twelve o'clock' position

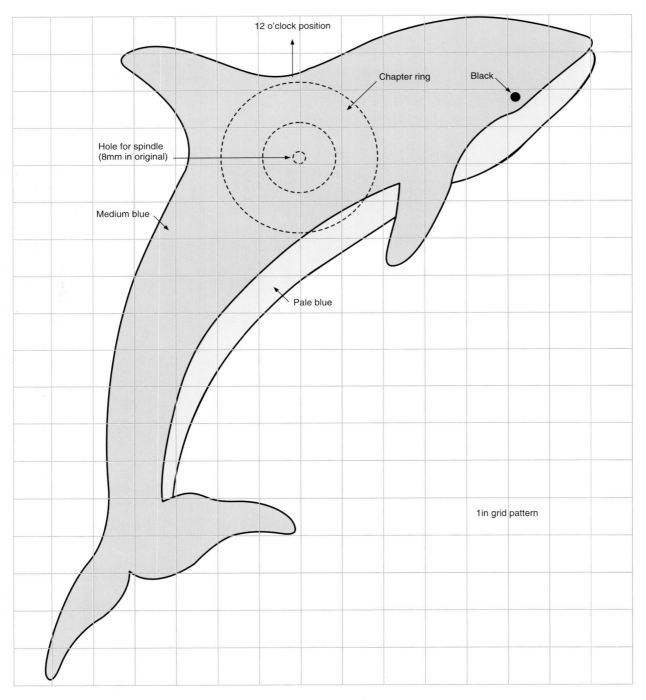

12 o'clock position

Chapter ring

Black

Hole for spindle
(8mm in original)

Medium blue

Pale blue

1in grid pattern

DOLPHIN CLOCK

Christmas characters

Ivor Carlyle brings you some super, fun decorations just for Christmas

These Christmas characters can be placed on the Christmas tree even taking the prime position at the top or suspended to provide window decoration and on walls. The shapes are very simple and can be easily scaled down on a zoom photocopier if smaller versions are required. They are ideal for using up those offcuts of softwood and plywood that would otherwise be thrown away.

I glued pieces of 19mm (¾in) x 69mm (2¾in) offcuts together to make up the necessary width and thickness required for the bodies. There is no reason why this cannot be varied to make use of whatever you may have to hand.

1 Wood ball drilling

To drill the wooden balls used for Rudolph and the turkey's head (see Patterns, Fig 1) make a jig which enables the drilling to be carried out accurately and safely by preventing the ball from rotating. Cut a hole the same diameter as the ball into a piece of MDF or plywood about 12mm (½in) thick. The ball sits in this hole, as can be seen in the photograph, with the exit cut from the hole parallel to the jaws of the drill vice. As the vice is tightened the exit cut is squeezed shut gripping the ball in place. It is now safe to drill the ball. When using the drill wear eye protection.

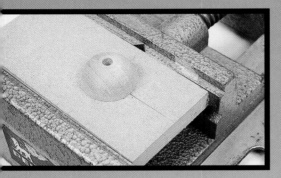

▲ Jig to enable wooden balls for Rudolph's head to be drilled

2

Mark up the hands, feet and boots (Fig 2) of the various characters onto the 19mm (¾in) pine and counterbore the 6mm (¼in) holes for the arms and legs before cutting out.

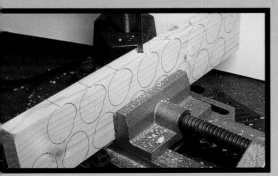

▲ Draw hands, feet and boots onto 19mm pine

When making the eyes, noses and beaks, shape the end before cutting to length.

3

When making the eyes, noses and beak (Fig 3) for the various characters from the 12mm (½in) dowel, first round off or shape the end before cutting to length. Note the use of a jig made from two pieces of scrap. A pin can be used as a stop to repeat the same cutting length.

4

Cut out the antlers (Fig 4), holly (Fig 5), turkey crest (Fig 3), Santa Claus hat rim (Fig 6) and turkey tail (Fig 7). If you are making

▼ Cutting out the antlers

several characters, stack layers of the plywood together with double-sided tape when cutting out the components. Round off to a 6mm (¼in) diameter section the stems on the antlers, holly and turkey crest with a sharp knife so that they will fit into their respective 6mm (¼in) holes in the top of their characters heads.

5

For the Xmas pudding mark up the body (Fig 5) and counter bore to a depth of 6mm (¼in) the

▲ **Drill holes for the nose and eyes**

12mm (½in) holes for the nose and eyes. Counter bore also the 6mm (¼in) holes for the legs and arms before finally cutting out the body.

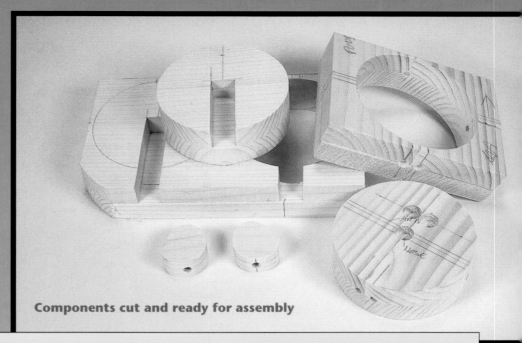

Components cut and ready for assembly

Cutting List

- 38mm (1½in) softwood
- 1 x pudding body 100mm (3¹⁵⁄₁₆) diameter
- 1 x Santa Claus body 135mm (5⁵⁄₁₆in) x 100mm (3¹⁵⁄₁₆in)
- 1 x Santa Claus hat 48mm (1⅞in) diameter
- 1 x Rudolph body 103mm (4¹⁄₁₆in) x 98mm (3⅞in)

- 19mm (¾in) softwood
- 1 x turkey body front 100mm (3¹⁵⁄₁₆in) diameter
- 1 x turkey body rear 100mm (3¹⁵⁄₁₆in) diameter
- 1 x turkey neck 112mm (4⅜in) x 40mm (1⁹⁄₁₆in)
- 2 x turkey feet 50mm (2in) x 48mm (1¹⁵⁄₁₆in)
- 6 x hands 34mm (1⅜in) x 32mm (1¼in)
- 2 x puddings feet 49mm (1¹⁵⁄₁₆in) x 30mm (1³⁄₁₆in)
- 2 x Santa Claus boot (leg) 44mm (1¾in) x 40mm (1⁹⁄₁₆in)
- 2 x Santa Claus boot (toe) 30mm (1³⁄₁₆in) x 40mm (1⁹⁄₁₆in)
- 2 x Rudolphs feet 41mm (1⅝in) x 33mm (1¼in)

- 6 mm (¼in) plywood
- 1 x turkey crest 39mm (1½in) x 33mm (1⁵⁄₁₆in)
- 1 x turkey tail 190mm (7½in) x 113mm (4⁷⁄₁₆in)
- 1 x pudding holly 94mm (3¹¹⁄₁₆in) x 45mm (1¾in)
- 1 x Santa Claus hat rim 66mm (2⁹⁄₁₆in) diameter

- 1 x Rudolphs antlers 138mm (5⁷⁄₁₆in) x 50mm (2in)

- 1.5mm (¹⁄₁₆in) plywood
- 1 x Santa Claus beard 58mm (2⁹⁄₃₂in) x 45mm (1¾in)
- 1 x Santa Claus buckle 40mm (1⁹⁄₁₆in) x 34mm (1⁵⁄₁₆in)

- 12mm (½in) dowel
- 1 x turkey beak 24mm (¹⁵⁄₁₆in)
- 2 x pudding eyes 12mm (½in)
- 1 x pudding nose 12mm (½in)
- 1 x Santa Claus nose 12mm (½in)
- 1 x Rudolph nose 12mm (½in)
- 1 x Rudolph neck 39mm (1½in)

Miscellaneous

- 2 x 37mm (1½in) diameter wood balls
- Crepe cord
- From craft or sewing and knitting shops
- Gumstrip
- 12mm (½in) picture frame screw eyes
- Oil based white primer
- Enamel paints. colours suggested pink, crimson, red, black, gold, tan, white, green and magenta
- Permanent liner pen for the facial features
- All gluing is with a PVA woodworking adhesive except where epoxy resin is specified

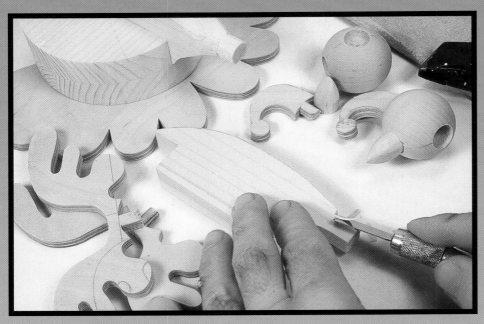

▲ Round off stems on antlers and crest with a sharp knife

6 For the turkey mark up the body front (Fig 3) with the slot on to a piece of 19mm (¾in) softwood. Cut out the slot only before gluing it to another piece of wood to make up the rear. When set, counterbore the 6mm (¼in) holes for the legs in to the body before finally cutting around the exterior line as seen in the top left of the photograph.

7 Cut out the turkey's neck (Fig 3) and with a knife, round off the top section that will fit into the head (Fig 1) to 12mm (½in) diameter and finally smooth off with abrasive paper and also round off the front edges of the neck.

8 Glue the tail (Fig 7) to the back of the body followed by the neck which is inserted into the slot in the body. Finally glue the beak and the crest on to the head and then glue the head on to the neck.

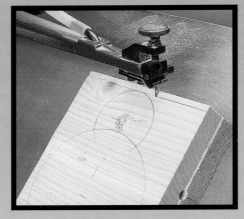

▲ Turkey body drawn onto 19mm softwood

9 Glue the eyes and nose into the holes in the pudding. Note that the holly is glued on after painting.

10 Mark up the Santa Claus body (Fig 6) and counterbore to a depth of 6mm (¼in) the 12mm (½in) hole for

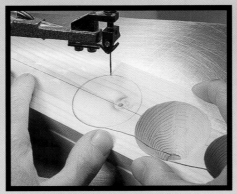

the nose and also the 6mm (¼in) holes for the arms and legs.

11 Cut a 45° bevel at the back of the head. This is at the saw's maximum capacity therefore you may find it hard going. If this should be the case alternatively cut by hand and level with a block plane. I used a No 9 wide-spaced tooth blade to avoid the soft dust and resin of the softwood from clogging in the cut. Finally cut out the body shape.

12 Mark up the hat (Fig 6) onto 38mm (1½in) thick wood and cut out at an angle of 25°. Smooth out the shape with

◀ Cutting out the body

▲ **Getting ready to cut internal details**

◀ **Components ready for assembly**

▼ **Attaching the legs**

abrasive paper and round off the pointed end.

13 Trim the bottom edges of the boot (leg) (Fig 2) section with the scrollsaw set at 45°.

14 Mark up the beard (Fig 6) onto 1.5mm (¹⁄₁₆in) plywood and drill 1mm (³⁄₆₄in) holes at the corners of the mouth. Insert a very fine blade through one of the holes in order to cut the slit for the mouth after which the blade is released. The same procedure is used for cutting out the buckle (Fig 6).

15 Mark up Rudolph's body (Fig 4) and counter bore the 12mm (½in) hole for the neck and the 6mm (¼in) holes for the arms and legs before finally cutting out the body as previously with the other characters. Glue the antlers (Fig 4) and the nose onto the head and join the head to the body with the neck dowel.

16 Glue the hat rim (Fig 6) to the top of Santa's head and the hat (Fig 6) onto the top of the hat rim. Glue in the nose and glue together the boot (leg) parts to the boot (toes) along with the other characters now awaiting painting.

Painting and finishing

17 Undercoat the wood with a white wood primer such as Japlac. Up to two coats may be necessary particularly with the open end grain areas of the softwood. I used gloss enamel paints to finish the characters.

I suggest using Japlac white primer and the Humbrol range of gloss enamels. These are all certified as safe for use with toys.

18 The dividing line between the white and plum coloured areas on the Xmas pudding and Santas Claus black belt are masked out with decorators tape to give a clean sharp edge.

19 The eyes and mouth lines can be added with a black permanent liner pen. The eyeballs of the Xmas pudding were masked out with tape that has had a hole made in it with a stationery punch. Double-sided tape placed on some bright red card and also punched out to make little dots were used as the berries on the holly on top of the pudding.

20 Santa Claus's buckle and beard are glued on with epoxy resin after the paint has been scraped to allow the adhesive extra grip.

21 Before cutting the crepe cord to length wrap pieces of Gumstrip around the cord where it will be cut. (Important, do not use self adhesive tape.) This prevents it from unravelling and makes the ends easier to insert into the holes in the characters' bodies when gluing in place. The turkey's legs need to be about 95mm (3¾in) long, Xmas pudding's legs 75mm (2¾in) long and Rudolph's and Santa Claus's 55mm (2⅛in) long while the arms are 60mm (2⅜in) long including the amount inserted in to the bodies. These lengths should be adjusted according to how deep you have drilled the holes.

22 Finally drill small pilot holes 1mm (³⁄₆₄in) diameter into the tops of the characters and fit in the screw eyes so they can be suspended with cords.

Wooden balls are obtainable from **Hobbies (Dereham) Ltd**, 34-36 Swaffham Road, Dereham, Norfolk, NR19 2QZ

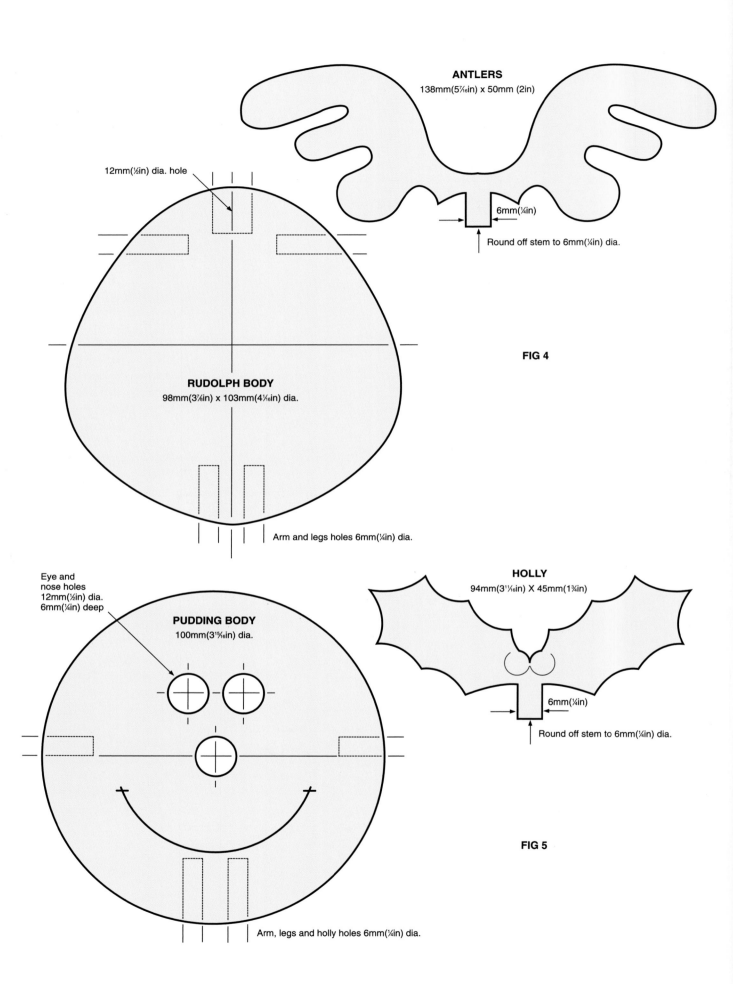

ANTLERS
138mm(5⅜in) x 50mm (2in)

12mm(½in) dia. hole

6mm(¼in)

Round off stem to 6mm(¼in) dia.

RUDOLPH BODY
98mm(3⅞in) x 103mm(4¼in) dia.

FIG 4

Arm and legs holes 6mm(¼in) dia.

Eye and
nose holes
12mm(½in) dia.
6mm(¼in) deep

PUDDING BODY
100mm(3⅝in) dia.

HOLLY
94mm(3¹¹⁄₁₆in) X 45mm(1¾in)

6mm(¼in)

Round off stem to 6mm(¼in) dia.

FIG 5

Arm, legs and holly holes 6mm(¼in) dia.

FIG 6

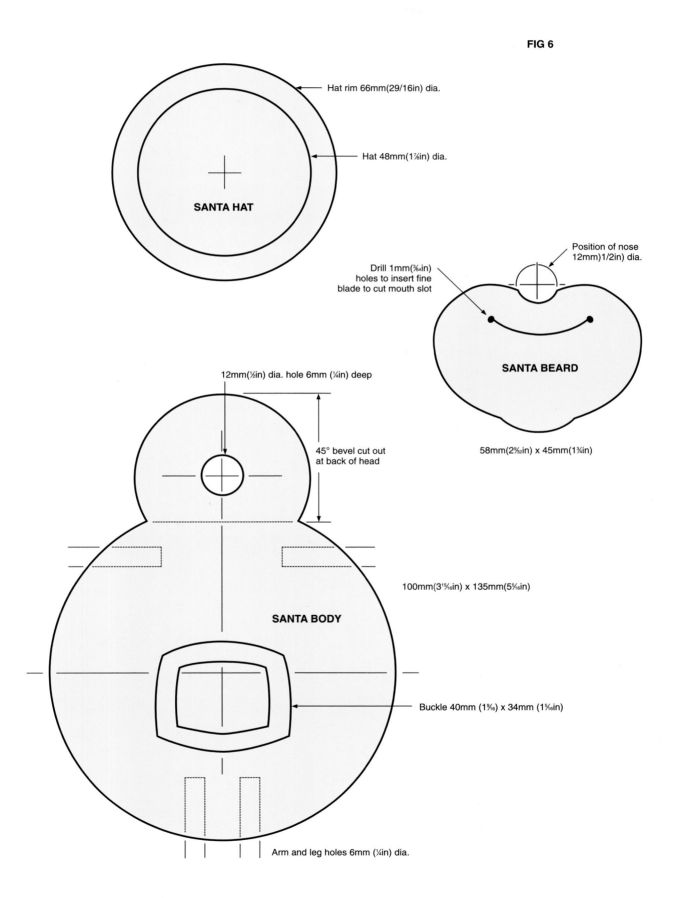

Hat rim 66mm(29/16in) dia.

Hat 48mm(1⅞in) dia.

SANTA HAT

Position of nose
12mm)1/2in) dia.

Drill 1mm(¾₄in)
holes to insert fine
blade to cut mouth slot

SANTA BEARD

58mm(2⅚in) x 45mm(1¾in)

12mm(½in) dia. hole 6mm (¼in) deep

45° bevel cut out
at back of head

100mm(3¹⁵⁄₆in) x 135mm(5⅜in)

SANTA BODY

Buckle 40mm (1⁵⁄₆) x 34mm (1⁵⁄₆in)

Arm and leg holes 6mm (¼in) dia.

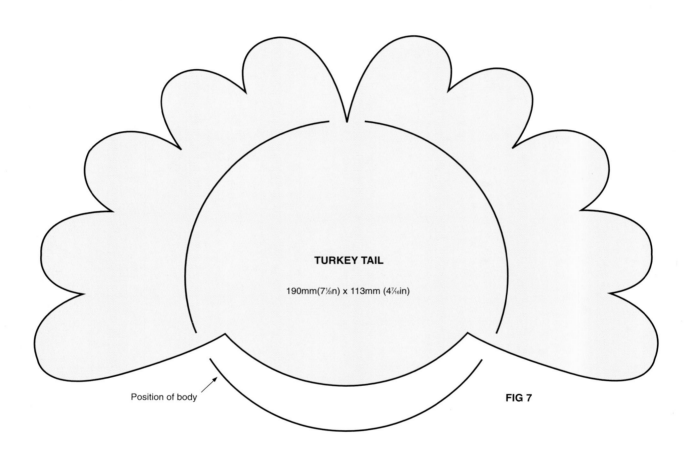

TURKEY TAIL

190mm(7½n) x 113mm (4⅞in)

Position of body

FIG 7

Tiers before bedtime!

The completed plant stand supporting part of a collection of bonsai tree and – sitting in the corner!

Here's an original space-saving idea for displaying your favourite items designed by **John Everett**

This item came about in answer to a request from my wife to design a multi-level stand for some of her collection of bonsai trees. Just to make things a little more awkward, she wanted it to fit on a corner shelf! Anyway, here is my answer to the problem. You can use this project for ornaments as well as plants just to make it a little more versatile.

The original shown here was made from two types of wood to provide a contrast in colour between the 'trays' and the support structure. Iroko from a 6mm (¼in) thick plank was used for the support structure and obeche which is paler - virtually cream - in colour, was used for the actual trays. You can of course, make this project in whatever type and thickness of material you happen to have to hand. Just bear in mind that the width of the slots which assemble the pieces need to be the thickness of the material you use.

There are no internal cutouts to make in this project, so sawing is straightforward from that point of view. You will need to take care to make the slots as accurate as you can and this is a good exercise in cutting straight lines to accurate dimensions with the scrollsaw. The project comprises the support, which is cut out in four pieces and three trays which carry the plants/ornaments or whatever takes your fancy. The trays have slots cut into them to fit over the projections on the supports and this feature ensures that the support struts are locked in place at exactly right angles for maximum strength and stability.

Materials

- 6mm sheet material. The one shown here was made from 6mm iroko. This material was bought from SL Hardwoods of London (tel. 0800 731 6345 for catalogue) as I don't have a planer/thicknesser to cut my own. You will need a piece of around 700mm x 180mm (27½in x 7in) for all the support parts.
- 8mm sheet material. Again, this was bought from SL Hardwoods and you will need obeche of some 500mm x 150mm (20in x 6in) for all three trays.
- A little double-sided tape will be useful to enable you to cut out all three trays together in one sandwich. Also some Spraymount adhesive and a small piece of sandpaper to clean away any saw tear out.
- You can add any decorating materials you think fit which will consist of just a coat of varnish if you are making this from wood, but paint or coloured varnish if you opt for MDF or ply as your material of choice.
- A set of cutting patterns copied to the size you wish to make your stand from the patterns given.

The other advantage of this method of construction is that there is no glue, nails or screws to fix anything together. This means that it will freestand on its own and when not required for use, can be packed flat and stored away in a drawer out of the way.

1 Lay out the cutting patterns for the individual parts of the plant stand to minimise ◀ wastage of your wood. Once you are happy with your arrangement, then stick the patterns down using Spraymount adhesive or similar.

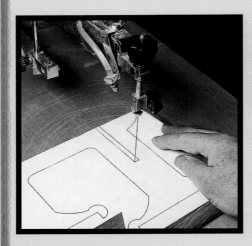

2 Begin by cutting out ▲ the slots on the support pieces. Make sure these are a good fit by following the cutting lines carefully. If you need to enlarge the width of the slots a little when you come to check them

for fit, use either a flat file or a strip of sandpaper glued onto a thin stick for the purpose and do it gently to avoid breaking the wood, especially if you are working across the grain. This will not be a problem if you have opted for making your plant stand in either ply or MDF of course.

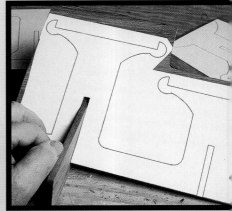

3 Once you have cut the ▲ slots which allow the individual pieces to slot together, check each slot with a piece of the same width material - perhaps an offcut from your cutting out - and adjust as necessary.

4 Once you are happy with the fit of the slots of all the pieces, you can carry on and make the remaining cuts so you have a complete set of support pieces. ▼

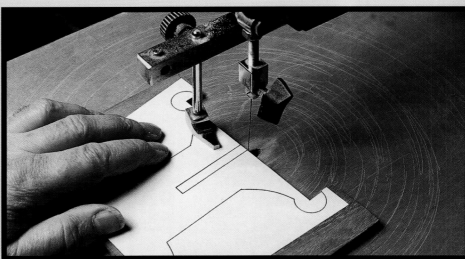

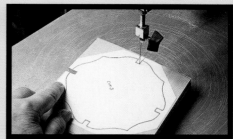

9 Begin sawing by ▲ cutting out the slots which will fit over the corresponding parts of the support pieces and will lock the support struts at right angles for maximum support.

5 The next step is to ▲ clean off any saw 'tear-out' from the backs of each piece and make a trial assembly to make sure everything fits together properly.

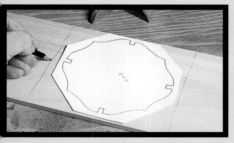

6 The next stage is to ▲ make up the trays that the plants will sit on. You will need three of these and as the wood used is quite thin, it is a good idea to make all three at once in a 'sandwich'. Mark out the wood using your cutting pattern so you can roughly cut out three blanks for the trays.

7 Use small pieces of double-sided tape to stick the three tray blanks together. By sticking each piece of tape outside the ▼

cutting line, which in this case will be in the corners, you will avoid having to carefully remove any residue of tape once you have finished cutting.

8 Assemble the blanks for all three trays into your stack and stick the cutting pattern in position with Spraymount adhesive. ▼

10 Once you have ▲ completed cutting out the trays, check them for fit on the assembled supports and adjust the slots as may be necessary.

11 You now have a completed plant stand with trays for plants on three levels and with the layout of the support pieces, you will find you can also fit this little stand into a corner if required. ▼

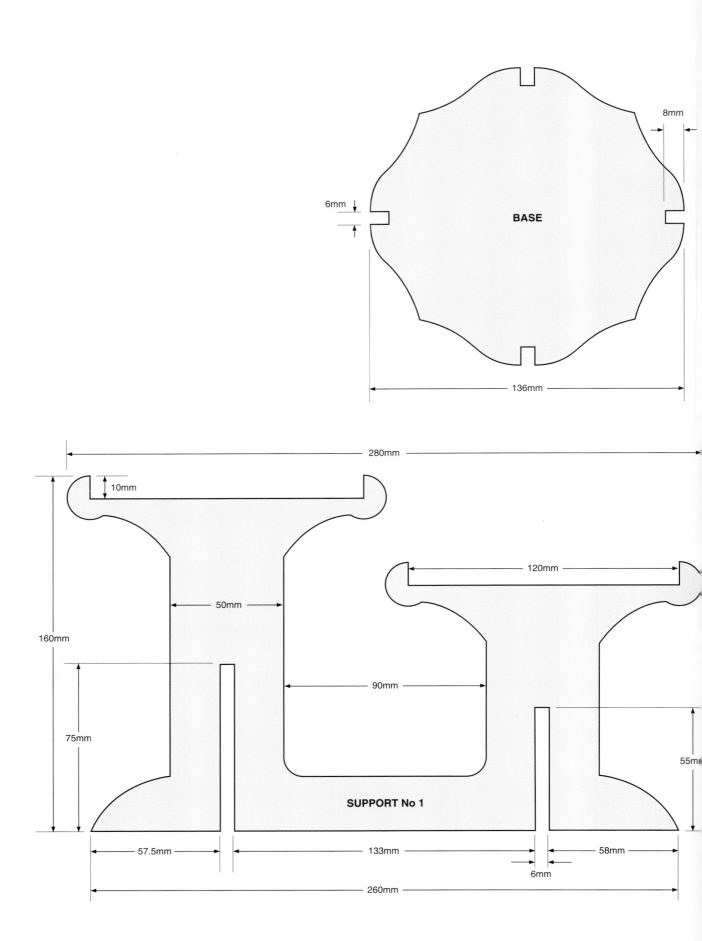

8mm

BASE

6mm

136mm

280mm

10mm

50mm

160mm

75mm

120mm

90mm

55mm

SUPPORT No 1

57.5mm

133mm

58mm

6mm

260mm

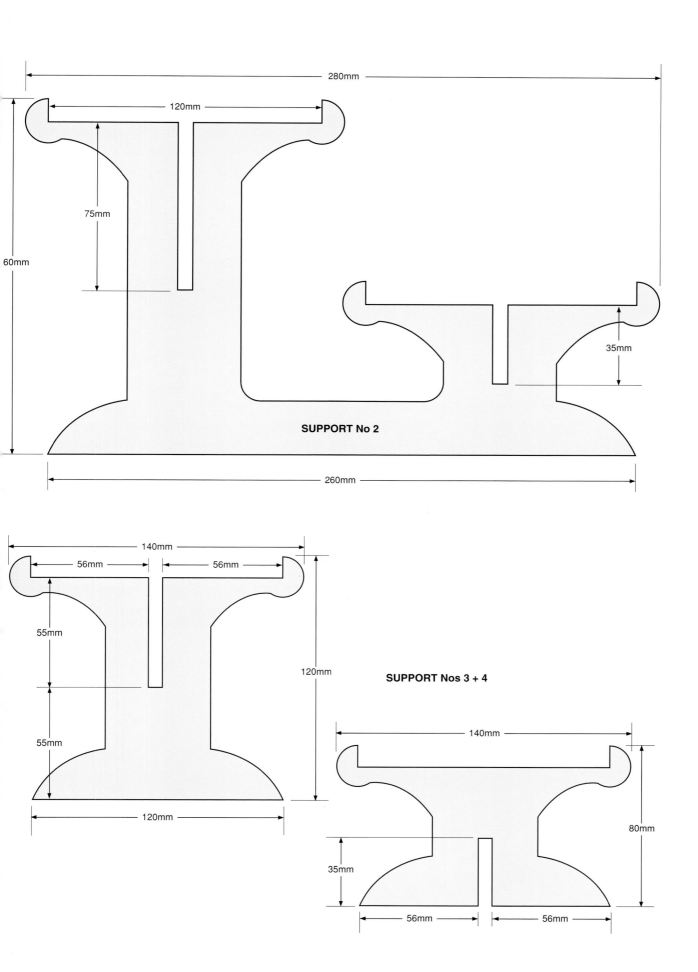

280mm

120mm

60mm

75mm

SUPPORT No 2

35mm

260mm

140mm

56mm

56mm

55mm

120mm

SUPPORT Nos 3 + 4

55mm

120mm

140mm

35mm

80mm

56mm

56mm

All the Kings

Tim Foxall designs an unusual, multi-purpose chess/draughts board and pieces

Chess can be a serious game, but you don't mind losing so much when using one of these sets. You can even complete the built-in jigsaw puzzle as well - the record is 9 minutes and 30 seconds from scratch. Different-shaped counters increase the artistic effect.

Marking out.

The lines must not be drawn on the wood itself. Draw on a separate square of paper and tape the edges to the two boards.

1 Draw out the borders.
a) Keep within a line 25mm (1in) from the outside.
b) Make sure that the lines A and B are in the directions shown (so that one bigger border is going to be cut off).
c) Do squiggly lines at both the corners, but make the rest of the lines vaguely straight. This is particularly important the further you get away from the corners: seven cuts are going to be made in each direction, and

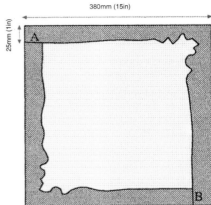

this means that the pieces are going to bunch up towards the corners and not be next to the matching grain/shape on the border.
d) Check that the inside square, the playing surface, is approximately square.

2 Subdivide each of the inside lines into eight (seven lines), making a mark at the edge. Don't measure it – use your eye to

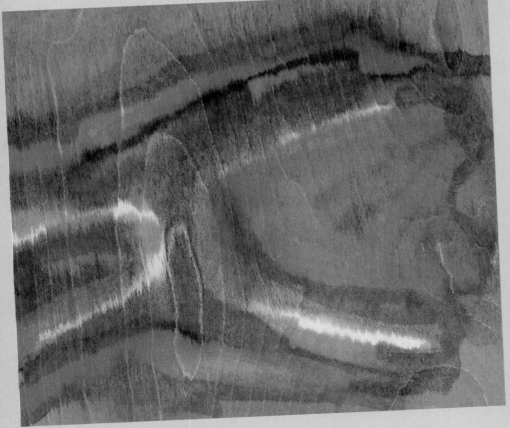

Chessboard before cutting up

Materials for boards (you make two at once):

4mm birch plywood: 2 @ 380mm (15in) square. Birch plywood really is important for this, providing a smooth surface that cuts smoothly and takes ink well.
Ink: it might be possible to just use one colour of light-fast acrylic ink, but I have never been able to persuade my students not to merge colours together. This also makes putting the jigsaw together easier (although jigsaw sky freaks might get a perverse sort of pleasure from matt light blue). Use lighter colours first and bleed other colours into them.

men!

divide each line in half, then into quarters and then eighths.

3 Draw light guide lines between opposite marks, checking that no square is too small. The diagonals should work out O.K., eliminating surprise attacks by bishops arriving out of the blue on boomerang trajectories.

4 It is important to remember that the chess board is also going to be a jigsaw. The first boards I made were like checkered flags, and therefore very difficult to put together. It is totally irrelevant for the jigsaw, but I now use lines that mean something to me, e.g. the No 23 bus route between Stirling and St. Andrews, the M 90, Scottish islands sticking up from the sea, things left in a pond, the Mississippi, the International Date Line, and numerous lines of music worked out by joining written music dots. For you, I suggest wavy lines in

one direction, and a mixture of the following lines in the other: zigzags: small waves: scallop pattern (loops): long waves: straight lines with interruptions: When drawing the lines in the opposite direction, the most important factor is to make sure that the lines cross each other at as near right angles as possible to

reduce the risk of corners breaking. Redraw details of the original lines if necessary. When cutting out the lines, you don't have to keep slavishly to the drawn lines.

Sawing and Assembly

Don't use too thin a blade for sawing the lines, and make sure that the blade is tight and vertical. This is because the checkerboard effect is created by taking pieces alternately from the two layers, and the pieces have to be similar in shape. The pieces will bunch together, and close fitting is achieved by sanding the edges at 'A' and 'B'. Reverse ground Olsen blades (No 5) are perfect because you don't have to sand the underneath of the base layer after sawing.

1 Nail the pattern and the two layers (with the grain going in opposite directions) together at the points marked 'X' with panel pins, as close as possible

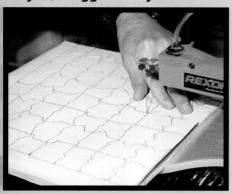

Saw along the lines

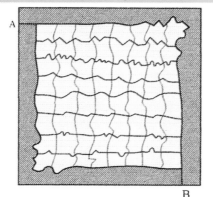

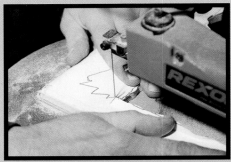

Continue sawing from where you left off

to the edge so that the holes can be sanded away afterwards. If only coping with the minimum two layers (rather than the six layers I wrestle with) it is possible to just tape them, either with Sellotape or double-sided tape, although check the effect on inked surfaces. However, it is so important that the layers don't move that pinning is best, certainly at 'C'. Saw off completely the larger border on the line 'AB'.

2 Saw the horizontal lines (marked in red), remembering to stop where indicated on the last one '8'. When you get to the end of each line, turn the saw off and wobble the saw blade back along the kerf (saw cut).

3 Saw the other lines 'a' to 'h', remembering 'a'. It is more important to cross lines at right

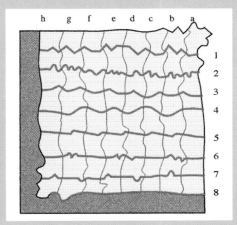

Push the jigsaw pieces together

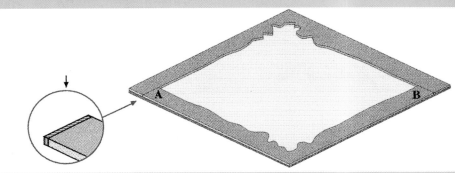

angles, to discourage splitting, than to keep exactly to the drawn lines.
b) Try not to cut into the border at the end of the line because the pieces are going to move along.
c) Stack the doubled jigsaw pieces in the right order on a side table after sawing off.
d) Start line 'h' from where you stopped sawing line '8'.

4 (Optional) Before gluing, draw a line parallel to the two edges that are going to be joined, not more than 2mm (7/64in) from the edge. Sand off carefully.

5 Glue the borders to the hardboard backing sheets, making sure that the borders meet together. I use a press, but you can use wood and clamps, or contact adhesive.

6 Saw/sand the edges square, making sure that you have got rid of any dribbled ink marks and panel pin holes.

7 Round off the corners (drawing round a small lid or similar as a guide), and neaten edges.

Chess pieces

8 Now for the exciting bit: put the jigsaw pieces in, taking them alternately from each layer of the

Assemble the two jigsaws using alternate pieces

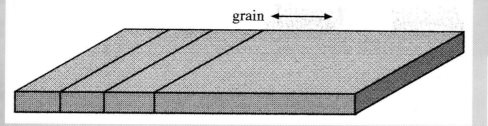

grain ←→

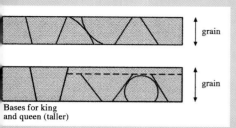

grain

grain

Bases for king and queen (taller)

neat pile on the side table. Do both jigsaws at the same time.

9 Depending on the ink used, spray varnish the boards.

Major Pieces – tops

I consider it *de rigeur* when designing a chess set that the pieces should be easily recognizable. It might not be immediately apparent, but this set is based on the standard Staunton pattern. In reality, I further plane/sand the plank to about 17mm ($^{11}/_{16}$in) for the tops of the pieces, but this is not essential. The tops should end up at between 20mm and 30mm diameter or square ($^{13}/_{16}$ and $1^{13}/_{16}$in).

KING: Drill 18mm (3/4in) holes, with centres 25mm (1in) apart, to about one-third of the depth of the wood. Cut out roundish shape, avoiding the pilot holes.

Materials List:

Contrasting hardwood planks, preferably walnut and sycamore, planed and sanded to about 20mm ($^7/_8$in) thick. At least 500mm x 200mm (20in x 8in), or equivalent, of each wood.
Alternatively you can make similar pieces from plywood, gluing horizontal layers together (3 for pawns, 4 for lesser characters, and 5 layers for kings and queens), and most of the slots for the tops can be cut out with a router, although they could be sawn and chiselled.

QUEEN: Drill 8mm (5/8in) hole to one-third depth. Cut out off-centre shape with the saw table at 15°.

BISHOP: Saw (or, preferably, use a router) a 3mm (1/8in) slot slanting at 15°. Cut out roundish shapes with the slot off-centre as in diagram.

CASTLE/ROOK: Saw and chisel (or rout, using a fence) 6mm (1/4in) slots to one-third depth, 35mm (1 1/4in) apart. Saw out vaguely squarish shapes, making sure that none of the projecting bits of the 'battlements' are too thin.

KNIGHT: Cut out the shape shown, turn on its side and then saw out an arc.

Pawns & Bases

1 Saw two 30mm ($1^3/_{16}$in) strips and one 36mm ($1^7/_{16}$in) strip from each of the two planks, across the grain.

2 Saw out the pawn and base shapes. At least half of them should have flat tops to make gluing easier later.

Stages for making the knight

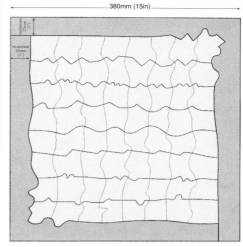

3 Round and sand the edges (including the tops), finishing with fine sandpaper. Keep the top and bottom edges parallel on at least half of the pieces so that you can glue the tops on flat. Also make sure that all the bottom surfaces are sanded flat to help with stability.

4 Glue on the tops, using an epoxy resin like 'Araldite'.

5 Coat all the chess pieces with Danish oil, remove the excess with a rag and leave to dry on absorbent paper. Buff up if required.

DRAUGHTS

The draughts are cut either from 6mm birch ply or thin pine, although they could be made from the same material as the chess pieces, but not more than 12mm ($^1/_2$in) thick.

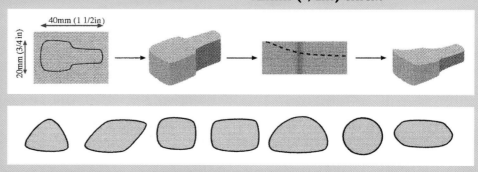

40mm (1 1/2in)

20mm (3/4 in)

Draught pieces out from 6mm ($^1/_4$in) ply

Fairy tale frame

Ivor Carlyle comes up with a novel idea for a photo frame

4 Separate the two pieces of plywood. Drill a hole in the 6mm (¼in) thick front and insert the scrollsaw blade and cut out the smaller of the two apertures indicated following the frame line and the top edge of the fungi where it overlaps.

5 Cut out the larger rectangular aperture from the 9mm (⅜in) back and also the slot for the prop.

Cutting list

- 6mm (¼) plywood
- 1 x front 220mm (8¹¹/₁₆in) x 187mm (7³/₈in)
- 1 x back insert 152mm (6in) x 105mm (4³/₁₆in)
- 1 x prop 66mm (2⁹/₁₆in) x 62mm (2⁷/₁₆in)

- 9mm (⅜in) plywood
- 1 x back 220mm (8¹¹/₁₆in) x 187mm (7³/₈in)

- 2mm (¹/₁₆in) acrylic glazing sheet
- 1 x glazing panel 152mm (6in) x 105mm (4³/₁₆in)

- Acrylic Gesso primer
- Acrylic hobby paints light blue, red, white, tan, brown, light grey, silver.
- Matt acrylic varnish

1 Trace or photocopy the frame outline with the fungi patterns. Stick the pattern on to 6mm (¼in) plywood with Spraymount.

2 Attach a piece of 9mm (⅜in) plywood to the back of the 6mm (¼in) plywood with double sided tape.

3 Cut out around the exterior outline of the frame and the fungis only. I used a No 7 blade.

Fly agaric (*Agaricineae Amanita muscaria*) is a particularly attractive fungi with the classic 'toadstool' appearance that everybody associates with woodland fairy tales. However it should be looked at and admired but not touched. It is extremely poisonous and even a hand that has only touched its surface and subsequently licked can cause some very unpleasant symptoms. However, this one is safe and can be displayed on the mantlepiece.

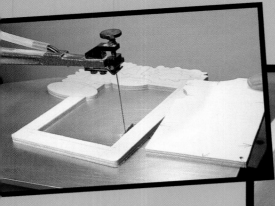

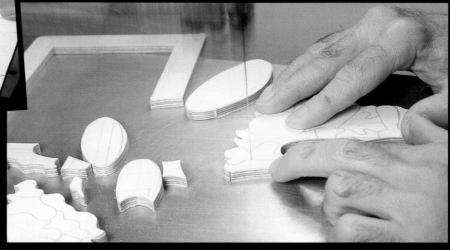

6 With a No 2 skip blade cut out the Fungi and leaf patterns from the front section.

7 To avoid confusion and mistakes mark the backs of the segments with a pencil before peeling off the paper template.

8 Round off the top edges of the pieces with a sanding block. A craft knife can be used to trim the edges of the straight sections.

9 Cut out a panel from 6mm (¼in) plywood or similar to make the back insert. I used an offcut of 6mm (¼in) MDF. Also cut a similar shaped piece from 2mm (¹⁄₁₆in) acrylic glazing sheet. Leave on the protective film and mount it on to a piece of thick cardboard with double-sided tape. Use masking tape on the top surface to provide a surface on which to mark the cutting lines. It also helps with cooling the plastic while cutting. I used a No 7 blade for this job.

10 All the parts are now ready for painting and final assembly.

11 Prime the edge of the back and the outer surfaces of the front with matt white artist's acrylic Gesso.

12 Paint the separate parts their various colours with matt hobby acrylic paints.

13 When the paint is dry glue the front segments to the back starting with the largest frame section using PVA wood adhesive. Also glue the prop in place in its slot in the back.

14 To provide extra protection to the surface of your photoframe you can give it a coat of matt acrylic varnish.

15 Peel the protective film from the acrylic glazing sheet and fit into the frame. After inserting the photograph the back insert is pushed into place.

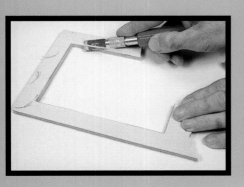

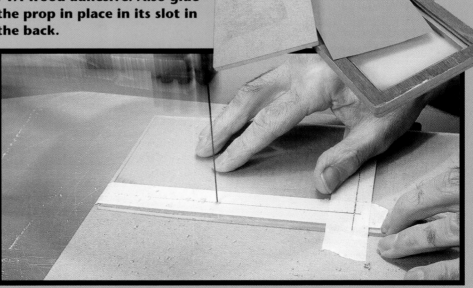

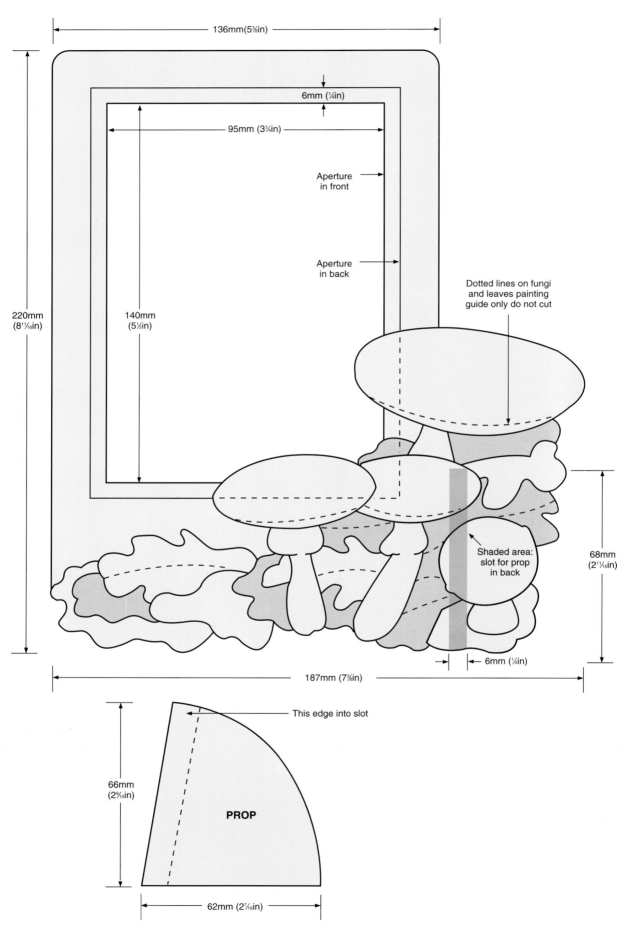

136mm(5⅜in)

6mm (¼in)

95mm (3¾in)

Aperture in front

Aperture in back

Dotted lines on fungi and leaves painting guide only do not cut

220mm (8¹¹⁄₁₆in)

140mm (5½in)

Shaded area: slot for prop in back

68mm (2¹¹⁄₁₆in)

6mm (¼in)

187mm (7⅜in)

This edge into slot

66mm (2⁵⁄₈in)

PROP

62mm (2⁷⁄₁₆in)

It's life Jim but!

Jeff Loader

shows you how to make these fantastic space-age rocket book ends

The finished bookends

I find it reassuring that in our high-tech and modern computerised age, children still adore reading books. My own two sons like reading exciting children's books as much as playing computer games (well....almost!), but they inevitably end up strewn across their room. After much persuading (and persistent nagging) they tend to put large books away in their bookcase, but their smaller books end up in the most unlikliest of places. I therefore designed these novel bookends to encourage them to store their books neatly on a shelf (I am ever the optimist!).

1 Stick two photocopied images of the main body of the rocket onto 12mm (¹/₂ in) birch plywood (or MDF). Spraymount adhesive is ideal for this task as it allows you to remove it readily later on. Then carefully cut these out with your scrollsaw, ensuring that the fin slot and 'cockpit' window are not neglected.

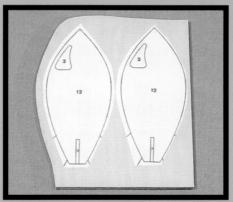

Two photocopied images of the main rocket body stuck onto 12mm (¹/₂ in) birch plywood

2 Transfer two images of the rocket's entire outline onto 3mm (¹/₈ in) birch plywood, paying particular attention to accurately reproducing the tail fins.

3 Carefully glue each rocket body directly onto the corresponding body areas of the rocket images

Materials

- I suggest that either birch plywood or MDF is used for the rocket and the uprights. A relatively heavy material needs to be utilised for the base. I suggest MDF, birch plywood or a 'weighty' hardwood and not a lightweight softwood such as pine (from DIY stores this is usually 'whitewood' spruce or fir)
- No 8 self-adhesive rubber 'feet' (available from good DIY stores)
- No 4 38mm (1¹/₂ in) countersink, crosshead, No 6 gauge screws
- No 2 50mm (2in) countersink, crosshead, No 6 gauge screws.
- Wood glue and child-safe paints

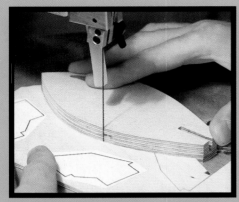

Cutting out the rocket and fin assembly

Using a sanding stick to smooth the edge of a rocket

reproduced on the 3mm (⅛in) birch plywood. Ensure that one cockpit window will be on the left side of one rocket and the right side on the other. Use heavy weights to hold these components together securely until the wood glue has set.

4 Cut around the rocket's body and the tail fins' outlines with your scrollsaw. Do not cut out the cockpit windows or the tail fin slots (only the 12mm (½in) plywood parts of these features are removed). Then 'clean up' any roughness or unevenness of the edges with assorted abrasive paper and sanding sticks.

5 Transfer two images of the front tail fin onto 3mm (⅛in) birch plywood and cut out.

Gluing a front fin into position

The image of the two uprights drawn onto 12mm (1/2in) birch plywood

6 Glue each front tail fin into its appropriate slot in the body of each rocket.

7 Transfer, or draw, the two uprights onto 12mm (½in) birch plywood or MDF. The decorative holes may be arranged in a pattern to suit you. Drill the holes, then cut around both

Drilling one of the decorative holes in an upright

Two MDF base blanks

upright's outline with your scrollsaw.

8 Prepare the two bases to the dimensions shown in the Patterns. Place each rocket onto a base and mark around each fin's tenon. The back mortices (tenon slots) should be approximately 8mm (⁵⁄₁₆in) in from the base's back edge.

9 Remove the waste from each fin's mortice in the bases. I removed the bulk of the waste by drilling a series of 3mm (⅛in) holes (use some form of a depth stop – a piece of sticky tape wrapped around the drill bit, to denote the fin's tenon depth, will suffice), then chopping out the

Marking the position of the fin tenons onto a base

The fin mortices marked out

remaining waste with a 3 and 6mm (¹/₈in & ¹/₄in) chisel. Ensure that each rocket's fins fit snugly and are not too tight, or too loose, a fit. Do not glue the rockets to their bases at this stage.

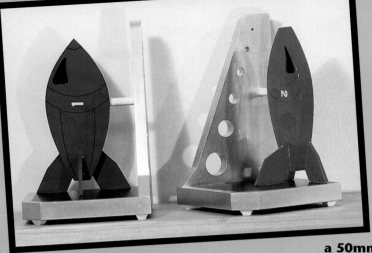

10 There are various ways in which you can join the uprights to the bases. I straightforwardly glued and screwed mine (two screws per bookend). I used 38mm (1¹/₂in) countersink, cross-head, No 6

Removing the 'waste' from a fin mortice

gauge screws of the twin-threaded variety that is suitable for man made boards like MDF. If using screws ensure that you drill suitable pilot holes and that you do not position a screw so that it will interfere with a tail fin mortice.

11 Fit (dry – no glue) each rocket onto their base. The covered 'gantry',

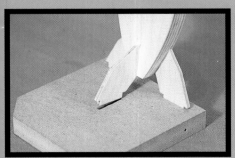

Testing that the fins fit correctly into the mortices

The finished bookends

from each rocket to upright, is in actual fact a 50mm (2in) countersink No 6 screw that is hidden by a short length of hard plastic tubing. This tubing is cut from a length of a biro pen's barrel! Each screw must be driven exactly into the centre of each rocket's side. Determine where the ideal position for each screw is, mark the point on each upright, remove each rocket, drill a shank clearance hole for

Securing an upright to a base with screws

each screw (4mm (⁵/₃₂in) diameter should suffice) and then countersink them on the outside (book side). You should find that the centre of the screw

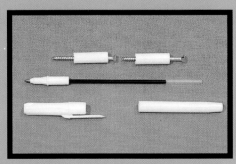

Rocket 'gantries' are constructed using a cut pen tube

hole is located approximately 95mm (3³/₄in) up from the top surface of the base and 15.5mm (⁵/₈in) in from the upright's back edge.

12 Re-fit each rocket to its base and place a 50mm (2in) 'gantry' screw through the appropriate hole in each upright. Ensure that the screw is straight and that it lightly indents its point into the rocket's side. This is the point in which the pilot hole must be drilled.

13 Remove each rocket from its base and drill the 'gantry' screw's pilot hole.

14 Reassemble each rocket bookend so that you can ascertain the exact lengths of pen tubing (barrel) required. Then cut the tubing to size using a fine-toothed saw (a junior hacksaw is ideal).

15 Paint the various components of the bookends. Ensure that you use paint that is suitable for children's toys.

16 Glue each of the rocket's fins into the base's mortices and fit each screw/tubing gantry.

17 Fit four self-adhesive rubber 'feet' to the underside of each base.

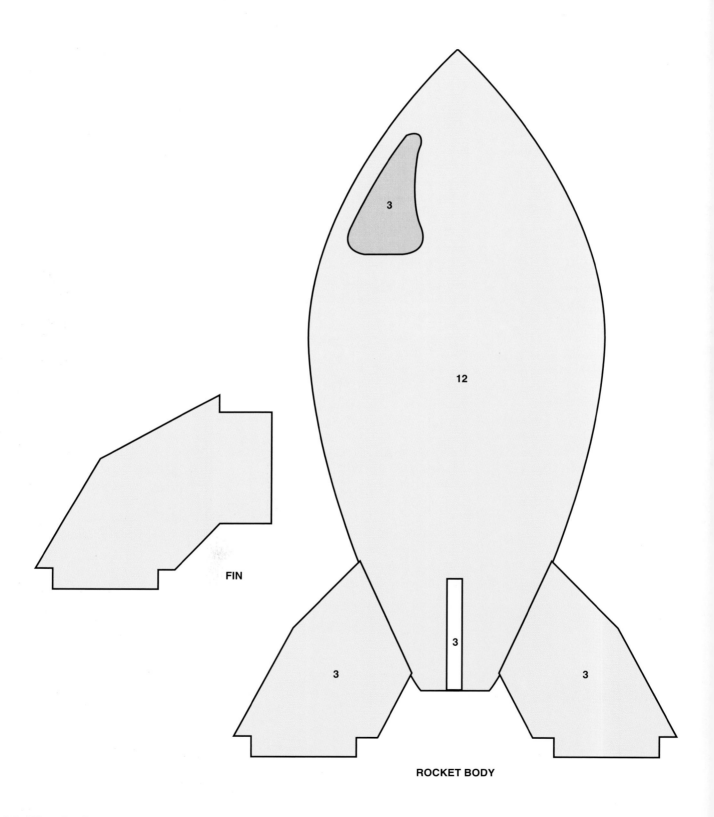

FIN

3

ROCKET BODY

Cook's organiser

The ideal solution to losing your favourite recipe is this useful kitchen accessory designed by **Ivor Carlyle**

I f you're like my wife and I you probably keep all your recipe cuttings and handwritten notes tucked into the pages of cook books and scrap books. I designed this organiser so various recipes can be stored within an A4 box which can be stacked on the shelf with the cookery books if wished. When a favourite clipping is required it can be retrieved from the box and laid between the transparent recipe cover and the box lid. The box can then be stood at an angle on the work surface to display the recipe by dropping down the flap at the back.

▲ **Recipes are protected and displayed for the cook to easily read**

Cutting List

• 6mm (¼in) birch multi-ply

1	Base	317mm (12½in) x 232mm (9⅛in)
2	Sides	330mm (13in) x 90mm (3⁹⁄₁₆in)
1	Top end	232mm (9⅛in) x 76mm (3in)
1	Base end	232mm (9⅛in) x 62mm (2⁷⁄₁₆in)
1	Flap	232mm (9⅛in) x 193mm (7⅝in)
1	Lid	310mm (12³⁄₁₆in) x 232mm (9⅛in)

• 1.5mm (¹⁄₁₆in) plywood

1	Top end lip	220mm (8²¹⁄₃₂in) x 56mm (2³⁄₁₆in)

• 4.5mm (³⁄₁₆in) hardwood dowel

1	Recipe cover pivot	232mm (9⅛in)

• 5mm (⁷⁄₃₂in) transparent acrylic

1	Recipe cover	318mm (12½in) x 232mm (9⅛in)

• Miscellaneous
3 x 12mm (½in) x 3mm (⅛in) self-tapping screws

1 Join two pieces of plywood together with double-sided tape and mark out the sides. Use a piece of plywood edge on to mark out the slots as shown in photo (see Fig 1 in Patterns) and drill out the pivot holes and the pilot holes for inserting the saw blade to fret out the slots before finally cutting out as shown in the photo. Fret out the slots cutting

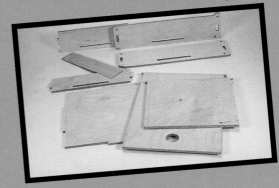

▲ **Plywood components marked ready for cutting**

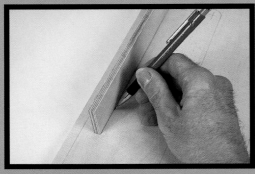

▲ Use a plywood edge on to mark out the slots

to the inside of the line. Cut out the other plywood parts. The finger hole in the lid is now fretted out as shown in the photo.

(When marking up the slots use a piece of the plywood being used edge on to the work to obtain the correct width and then cut to the waste side of the lines for an accurate fit.)

▲ Round off the rear pivot edge of the flap with a plane

2 With a plane round off the rear pivot edge of the flap. The inner sides of the pivots are whittled out with a knife and the whole pivot area is then rounded off with a sanding block. Check the pivots for fit with the 6mm (¼in) diameter holes in the sides until a smooth accurate fit is achieved. Smooth off the sharp edge of the bevel also.

▲ Drill pilot holes for inserting saw blades

3 Shape the pivot area on the lid (Fig 2 in Patterns) in the same way as described in step 2.

4 Glue the top end lip to the top end as shown by the shaded area in Fig 1 in Patterns.

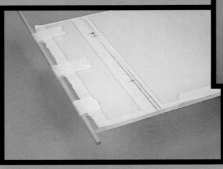

▲ Bind tightly with masking tape and leave glue to cure

5 Cut out the recipe cover (see Fig 2 in Patterns) from 5mm (³/₁₆in) acrylic sheet. Use masking tape applied to the surface of the acrylic sheet to aid marking up and to aid cutting as shown in the photo. Note: sticking the acrylic to a piece of scrap ply or hardboard with double-sided tape will

▼ Fret out the slots, cutting to the inside of the line

assist cutting. Slightly flatten one side of the pivot dowel with a sanding block and then with epoxy resin glue the flattened edge to the hinge end of the recipe cover. Bind on tightly with masking tape and leave to cure and harden. Clamp the recipe cover firmly in a Workmate and drill three 3mm x 12mm holes through the hinge dowel and into the acrylic. I used a hand-held cordless drill. Cover the threads of the screws

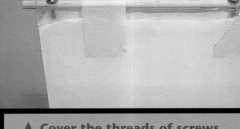

▲ Cover the threads of screws with epoxy resin and place in holes

with epoxy resin and place them in to the holes. A blast of warm air from a hairdryer will assist in making the adhesive flow. Wipe off the excess resin with methylated spirit. Note: scratches can be polished away from acrylic with automotive paintwork rubbing compound or Brasso metal polish.

▲ The finger hole is cut out

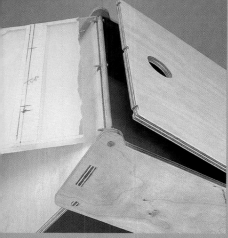

▲ Check recipe cover and lid for proper opening

▲ Use masking tape to aid marking up and cutting

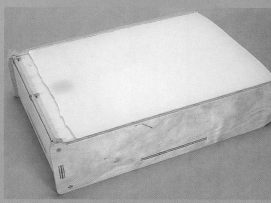

▲ Rub down inner surfaces before gluing and assembling

6 Dry assemble all the parts and check for fit. The top end fits the end of the sides which has the holes for the flap and recipe cover. The base end fits the other end. Note: the bevel on the flap must face towards the base. Apart from being the correct position it also aids its opening. Mark up on the upper edge of the top end the positions of the screw heads on the recipe cover. Do the same on the lid. Dismantle and cut out the notches in the top end and the lid. Reassemble and check that the recipe cover and lid open properly.

7 Rub down the inner surfaces before gluing and assembling. Make sure all the pivots are candle waxed before fitting to ensure a smooth hinge action. Bind the box together with tape and clamp well while glue sets.

8 After smoothing all surfaces with grade 220 aluminium oxide abrasive paper the box can be varnished. Keep the recipe covers protective film in place until everything is finished. A satin acrylic varnish is ideal and is non-toxic. It is possible to blend acrylic hobby paints (Humbrol for example) with the varnish to a ratio of about one part paint to five parts acrylic varnish. Test the mix on a piece of scrap plywood to check the result and adjust if necessary for the result required before applying the first coat. Rub over gently with grade 220 abrasive and apply a second coat of the varnish.

▲ The inside of the organiser can hold all sorts of cooking appliance instructions, recipes and notebooks

Suppliers

5mm (7/32in) acrylic sheet can be obtained as small offcuts from J. B. Hindley Ltd, 26B Lion Works, Ball Street, Sheffield S3 8DB, tel 0114 278 7828, fax 0114 278 8558. Also from specialist glaziers, coach builders and commercial sign companies.

Acrylic varnish with a gloss, satin and matt finish is made by Rustins Limited and if unobtainable locally can be obtained from Axminster Power Tool Centre. Telephone 01297 33656.

1.5mm (1/16in) plywood and 4.5mm (3/16in) dowels are obtainable from Hobbies (Dereham) Ltd. Telephone 01362 692985.

The organiser can be stacked up with the cookery books

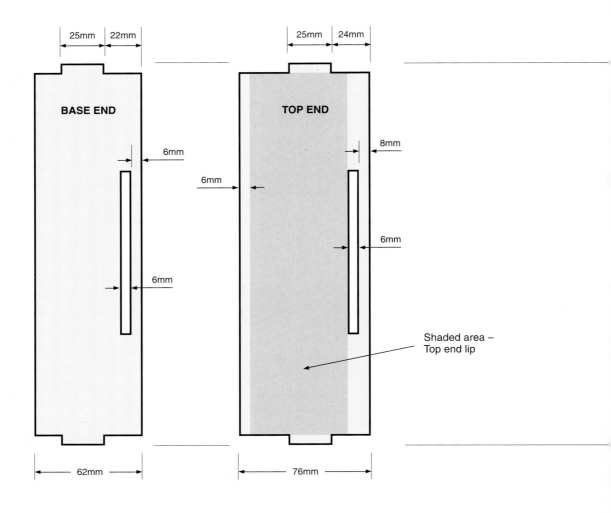

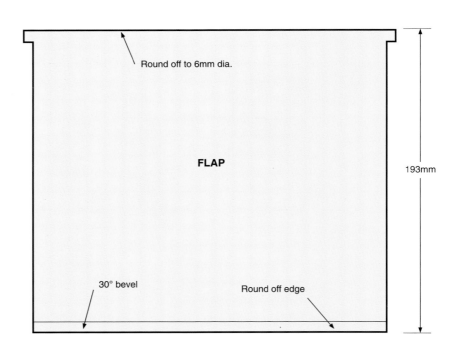

BASE END

TOP END

25mm | 22mm

25mm | 24mm

6mm

8mm

6mm

6mm

6mm

Shaded area –
Top end lip

62mm

76mm

FLAP

Round off to 6mm dia.

193mm

30° bevel

Round off edge

FIG 2a

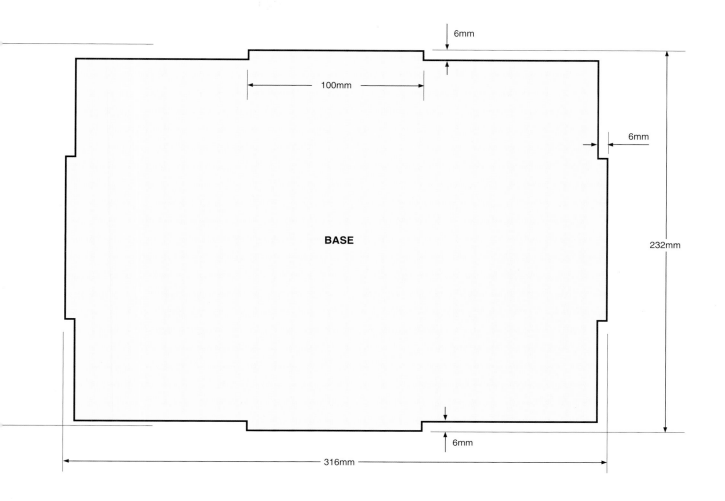

BASE

6mm

100mm

6mm

232mm

6mm

316mm

FIG 1

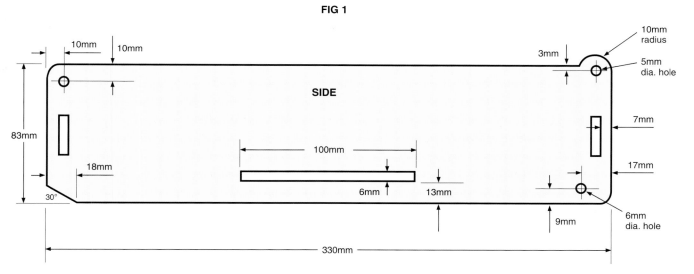

10mm radius

10mm   10mm

3mm

5mm dia. hole

SIDE

83mm

7mm

100mm

17mm

18mm

6mm   13mm

30°

9mm

6mm dia. hole

330mm

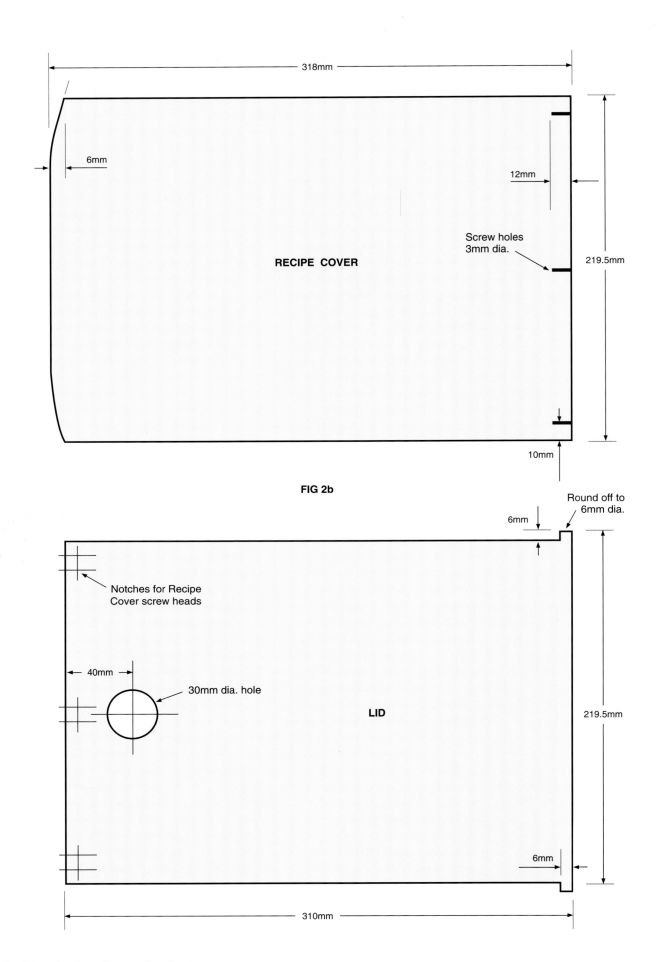

318mm

6mm

RECIPE COVER

12mm

Screw holes
3mm dia.

219.5mm

10mm

FIG 2b

Round off to
6mm dia.

6mm

Notches for Recipe
Cover screw heads

40mm

30mm dia. hole

LID

219.5mm

6mm

310mm

Blow your horn

Make a table-top music stand for your budding musicians
Project and photography
Christine Richardson

Whatever the instrument your favourite musician plays, this stand will be a great help. If you are feeling creative you can even adapt the design to feature a different instrument, it's not hard as you only need the outline. This table-top version saves you tripping over the tripod base of traditional floor-standing designs and can be used to support cookery books or knitting patterns too, so what are you waiting for, someone near you needs this project.

Materials

- 2 @ 12mm x 250mm x 450mm birch ply
- 1 @ 12mm x 40mm x 450mm birch ply
- 20cm brass-plated decorative chain
- 2 x screw eyes
- 4 x rubber feet
- 2 x brass butt hinges 50mm long
- 20mm panel pins
- Quick-setting wood glue

Tools

- 10 tpi skip tooth reverse blade for straight lines
- 20 tpi spiral blade for curved lines
- Hammer
- 2mm drill bit
- Electric drill/screwdriver
- 240 grade abrasive paper or electric palm sander
- 2 x pair of pliers
- Bradawl
- Pencil

1 Transfer the template for the front and back supports to your timber.

2 Mark all the waste areas of the design, that are to be cut. Drill a hole in each of these waste areas. Waste areas with corners should have a hole drilled in each corner; it gives the blade somewhere to escape to for turning the work around.

3 Clamp the spiral blade in the lower jaw and thread the blade through one of your drilled holes. Clamp the blade in the upper jaw and tension the blade. You are going to cut only the curved lines with this blade and complete the cutting out of any waste areas with straight lines with the skip tooth blade.

4 Follow and cut all the curved lines in each waste area, this can take some time on a design of this size, so take a few breaks from the work to rest your back.

5 Once all the curved lines and outside corners are cut on your front panel, don't forget to cut the inside and outside corners of the back panel before changing to the skip tooth blade, remember to de-tension and re-tension the blade when changing it.

6 With the skip tooth blade fitted and threaded through one of the waste areas of your design, finish sawing the straight lines of the design. This blade gives a really clean cut, but it is quite fragile and won't take much abuse so remember not to push too hard. If you need to change direction, stop the machine and turn the work rather than push

the blade in the wrong direction.

7 When all the fretwork is complete, sand all faces of the timber using the palm sander; remember to sand with the grain. It is alright to slightly round over the outside edges of the supports and the design, so don't worry about keeping the palm sander or sanding pad at right angles. However, the back edge of the shelf where it is attached to the front of the stand must be kept crisp to aid fixing. Use a scrap of abrasive paper to sand the fretwork, which has to be done from both sides. When you are happy with the finish the stand is ready for assembly.

Assembly

8 Lay both supports face down with top edges facing inwards, ensure that both pieces are

aligned and leave a small gap between them to accommodate the butt of the hinge. Measure an equal distance of around 60mm from each outside edge and mark the work. Lay the hinges face upwards at these marks. Use a pencil to mark the position for each screw. Drill the holes but don't screw on the hinges yet.

9 Glue along the back edge of the shelf and if clamps are available use these or masking tape to keep it in the correct position while you fix it with panel pins. Turn the work over supporting the panel and hammer the pins through the back of the front panel into the back edge of the shelf. Once the pins are in, remove the clamps or masking tape.

8 Drill holes in the base of the front and back panels for the feet, and attach the feet. Screw on the hinges.

9 The chain that stops the stand opening fully, is held at each end by screw eyes. Use a bradawl to start the holes for these, then screw in by hand.

- Check blades are properly tensioned by strumming the back of the blade with your thumb; if it rings with a pleasant note your blade is tensioned, if it dings try adding a fraction more tension.

- If you are restarting the machine with the blade in a saw cut, hold the timber down as you turn on, this prevents the timber jumping.

- Blades that are too weak for the thickness of timber you have chosen will wander in the cut, this will also happen if your blade is not under sufficient tension.

- The spiral blade will cut a wider and coarser saw line than the skip tooth blade which is very fine.

- Decide where you are going to make your cut before you start the machine. You have a choice of cutting on either side of a drawn line or actually on the line itself. Most of us find that one side of the line is easier to cut on than the other, related to left- or right-handedness, once you know which you find easiest, try turning the work so that your preference works for you.

Use two pairs of pliers to open the links of the chain to attach it to the screw eyes, and then to close the links again.

Finishing

10 You have three basic choices of finish available to you; stain, varnish or paint. The finish used here is rosewood spirit stain, sealed with satin quick-drying varnish for a traditional look. There are a number of varnishes available with stain added, and of course the choice of paint colours are unlimited. The latest trend is for metallic paint which is usually acrylic and easy to apply. Spirit stain can be brushed on or rubbed on with a rag, but wear rubber gloves because it really does stain everything! Don't worry about overlapping strokes, unlike some finishes this one is quite forgiving, just aim to work quickly, in one direction and to apply one coat only. Leave to dry, wipe off splashes on the hardware and then varnish. Quick drying varnish is dry in around two hours depending on the manufacturer.

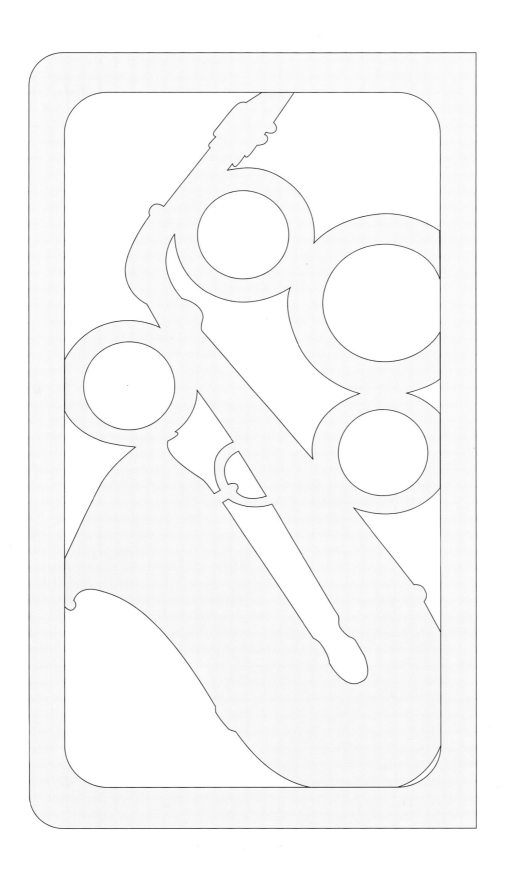

Inventive building

Bringing fun and enjoyment to an old favourite, **Terry Lawrence** re-designs the building block

◀ A palace made with blocks showing their yellow faces

My children still remember with pleasure their first sets of wooden bricks, 35 years after I made them. So I thought it was time to try another set, especially as most children's bricks are now in hard plastic with limited variations.

Commercial bricks, both wooden and plastic, are frequently rather garish, with the child left to put together, say yellow and purple, or other colour discords.

I thought it a good idea to build in colour harmony using adjacent hues on the colour circle, and I decided first to make the Hot Lot, a collection using yellow, orange and red. Later a companion set could be the Cool Collection using green, blue and turquoise.

A typical piece of the Hot Lot features one face on yellow, the reverse in red and the ends and edges in orange.

The orange colour is introduced on the faces of the flat shapes by cutting optional recessed grooves. Your child can then mix

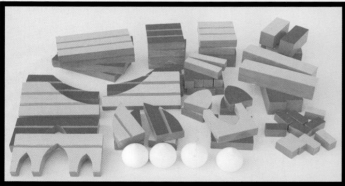

▲ The full set   ▼ The 12 basic shapes

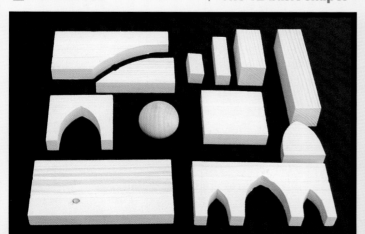

▲ Full set of 60 pieces

◀ Trees and bushes, cut from plywood

MAKING SQUARE PIECES

I have made just four sizes:
- 32mm (1¼in) square, 150mm (6in) long. *Quantity 4*
- 32mm (1¼in) square, 75mm (3in) long. *Quantity 4*
- 18mm (¾in) square,75mm (3in) long. *Quantity 10*
- 18mm (¾in) square, 37.5mm (1½in) long. *Quantity 10*

Method

1 Cut the larger pieces from the 32mm (1¼in) square planed all round timber and sand smooth the ends. These ends will need sealing as end grain, especially softwood, will absorb paint and still remain rough, sanding sealer or primer will both work to seal the ends. I chose to use a white acrylic wood primer which dries in an hour.

2 When dry, sand all over with fine abrasive (180–240 grit). It is a good idea to repaint the end grain with a second application at this stage.

3 You may now apply the colours. I used non-toxic paints: one small, 125ml tin each of red and yellow will be sufficient. Be careful when mixing the orange (use a separate container) not to overdo the red. Take about six tablespoons of yellow and one half-teaspoon of red and mix thoroughly. You can then adjust the hue if necessary.

4 First apply the orange to opposite long sides and the ends. Leave to dry flat on an unpainted side, preferably overnight. Then you can paint one long side yellow. When dry, finish with red on the last long surface.

---

and match, and every model built can be in three colourways or a mixture of the three.

Convenient materials

Most wooden bricks are made from hardwood, but many people do not have ready access to supplies, so this set of bricks is made from softwood which is readily available at any DIY store.

I selected a module of 75mm (3in) which can be doubled, halved or quartered at will. I chose ordinary white pine of 18mm (¾in) thickness for all the flat pieces, and 32mm (1¼in) square for the largest square sectioned pieces.

I found that 12 shapes and a total of 60 pieces were adequate, but you can make more or fewer. I added four domes in ash that I turned on a lathe and painted white. If you don't have a lathe then just cut their profile from 18mm (¾in) timber.

The 60-piece set, illustrated, cost about £9 for the timber. All the cutting was done on a scrollsaw and the pieces were finished on a disc sander, but you can use a hand sanding block for equally good results.

I cut out and sanded smooth all the 60 pieces in one session of just under four hours. The painting took longer!

FLAT PIECES

I found five sizes sufficient, plus the cut-outs from the gateway pieces, and the quadrants from the large, top-curved wall sections (seven shapes in all).

- 75mm x 75mm x 18mm (3 x 3 x ¾in) plain. *Quantity 8*
- 75mm x 75mm x 18mm (3 x 3 x ¾in) with door cut-out. *Quantity 2*
- 75mm x 150mm x 18mm (3 x 6 x ¾in) plain.*Quantity 4*
- 75mm x 150mm x 18mm (3 x 6 x ¾in) with 3 gateways with cut-out. *Quantity 2*
- 75mm x 150mm x 18mm (3 x 6 x ¾in) with quadrant 100mm x 50mm (4 x 2in) cut out. *Quantity 4*

Shapes 1, 3 and 5 have two grooves on each flat side running along the grain. Shape 4 has one groove on each side.

Method

1 Either trace the curved lines onto your timber using carbon paper or more easily, make cardboard templates and cut the shapes on a scrollsaw.

2 Discard the small doors cut from shape 4 as they are small enough to present a hazard to a small child.

3 The grooves are optional, but they do relieve what would otherwise be plain surfaces. Mine were cut to a depth of 3mm (⅛in) using a miniature router. The centre of the groove was set 25mm (1in) in from the edge. If you do cut grooves, it is best to do so before cutting out quadrants or the gateways.

4 Make the quantities that you require of each shape, then sand, prime, sand and re-prime.

5 Painting the pieces is similar to the procedure outlined above with a couple of variations.

a Paint the grooves first, using a small (No 2 or No 3) artist's prolene or squirrel-hair brush. These sizes will fit inside the groove and can be trailed along the groove pushing the paint up to the top edges of the groove. Don't worry if you go over the top – you can scrape the surface when it is dry with a sharp knife.

b With shape 5 paint these as two matched pairs in mirror image (and do the same with their quadrant cut-outs too). This preserves the colour scheme if you use these pieces on either side of a doorway, for example.

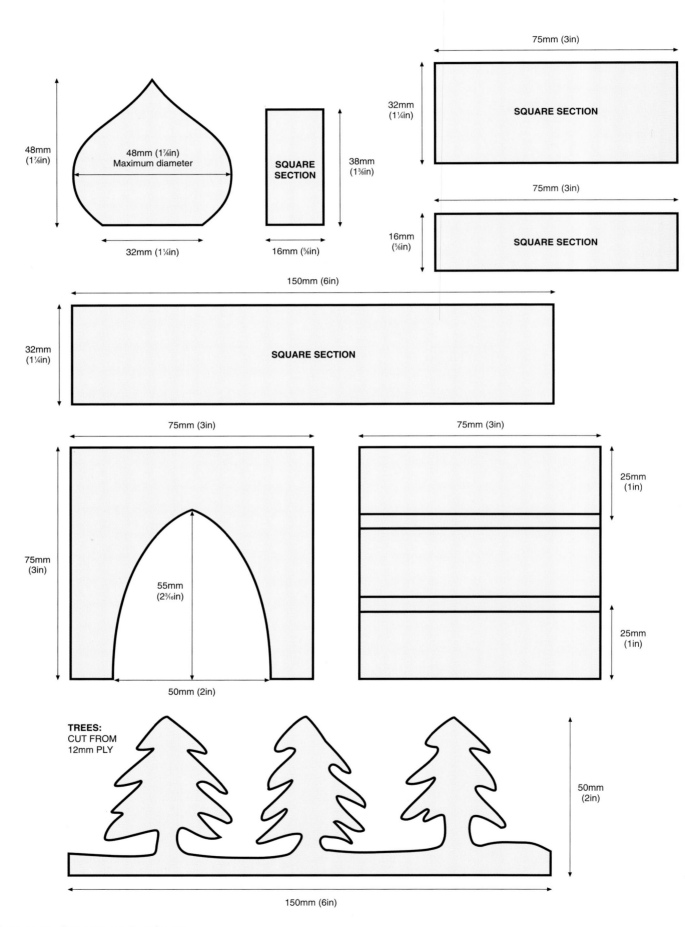

48mm (1⅞in)

48mm (1⅞in)
Maximum diameter

32mm (1¼in)

SQUARE SECTION

38mm (1⅜in)

16mm (⅝in)

75mm (3in)

32mm (1¼in)

SQUARE SECTION

75mm (3in)

16mm (⅝in)

SQUARE SECTION

150mm (6in)

32mm (1¼in)

SQUARE SECTION

75mm (3in)

75mm (3in)

75mm (3in)

55mm (2³⁄₁₆in)

50mm (2in)

25mm (1in)

25mm (1in)

TREES:
CUT FROM
12mm PLY

50mm (2in)

150mm (6in)

58 Simple Scrollsaw Projects

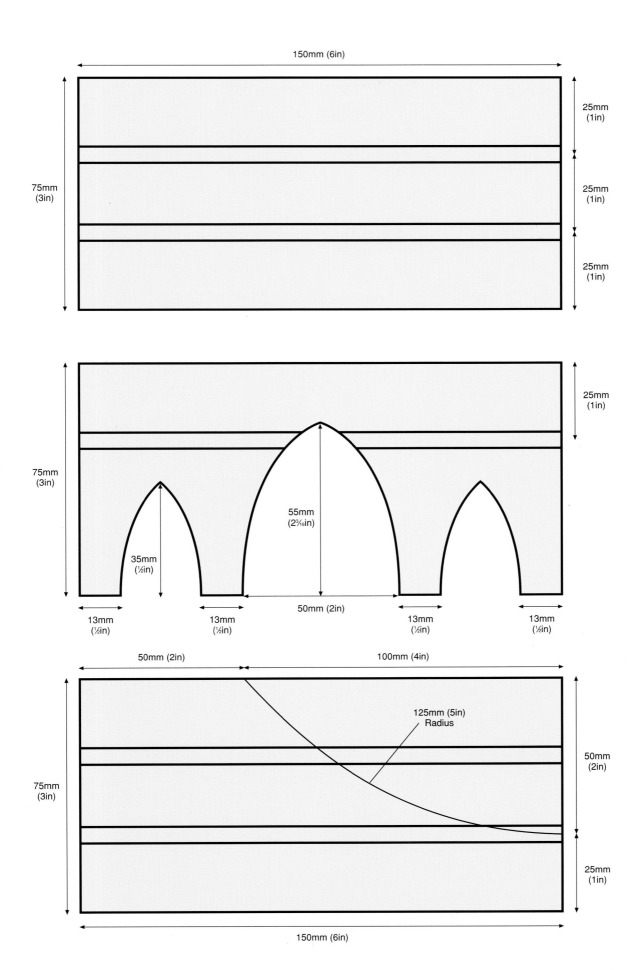

150mm (6in)

25mm (1in)

75mm (3in)

25mm (1in)

25mm (1in)

25mm (1in)

75mm (3in)

55mm (2³⁄₁₆in)

35mm (½in)

13mm (½in)

13mm (½in)

50mm (2in)

13mm (½in)

13mm (½in)

50mm (2in)

100mm (4in)

125mm (5in) Radius

50mm (2in)

75mm (3in)

25mm (1in)

150mm (6in)

Sails Ahoy!

A yachting theme is the basis for this original bathroom design by **Christine Richardson**

Make the towel rail and toilet roll holder, and later in the book we show you how to make a matching bathroom mirror

Using the original design in the pages which follow, we show you how to make a three-part set of bathroom accessories. The towel rail and toilet roll holder are easy to saw on your scroll saw, while the chunky timber we've used gives them an extra dimension. The painting is easier still and will give you perfect results; why not choose colours to tie in with existing decorations and linen?

1 Photocopy and enlarge the templates on the following pages. Cut around the outline and stick them to your timber with repositionable Spraymount. Repeat all steps for both the towel rail and the toilet roll holder.

2 Saw along the lefthand outline.

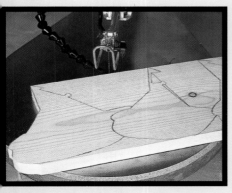

▲ Separate the towel rail from the toilet roll holder

Materials

- 170 x 20mm (6¾in x ¾in) prepared pine
- 25 x 135mm (1in x 5⅜in) dowel
- 4 x 30mm (1⅛in) beech wood knobs
- 240 and 150 grade abrasive paper
- 3 mirror plates
- 1 metre 8mm (3ft x ⁵⁄₁₆in) rope
- Variety of emulsion test pots
- Quick-drying clear matt varnish

Tools

- 10 tpi blade for 25–50mm (1in–2in) timber
- 2B pencil
- Bradawl
- 2mm drill bit
- 10mm lip & spur drill bit

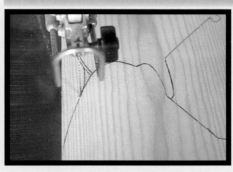

▲ Negotiate inside corners by sawing into the corner then backing up and leaving waste to be removed later

3 Saw along the outline of the bottom of the boats and then continue to the sails and masts. As you approach inside corners, continue the cutting line into the corner, back the blade up a couple of millimetres into the line just sawn and gradually realign to a less acute angle, this may mean allowing the blade to nibble the wood, while you turn the timber gradually without pushing it onto the blade. Carry on the cut and regain the line after the corner.

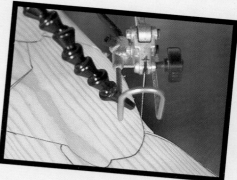

▲ Remove the waste from an inside corner with a second cut, after the majority of the waste area has been removed

4 When the majority of waste has been removed, return to the small amount of waste left in the corner and approach it from the opposite side cutting along the line to meet the first cut in the corner.

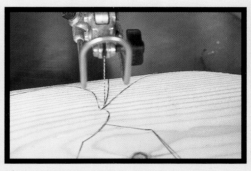

▲ An alternative way to tackle inside corners is to make a saw line into the centre, the waste area on each side is then divided in half

5 If the corner seems too acute, make a central saw cut straight to the corner and then make two more cuts along the outline from opposite directions, to remove the waste area on each side.

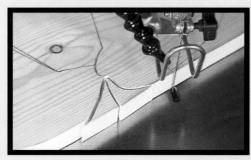

▲ Cuts are made from both directions towards an inside corner and join up with the previously sawn central line

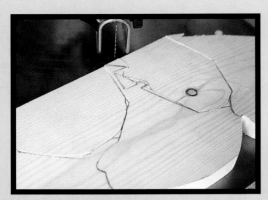

▲ Large areas of waste can be sawn off with one pass

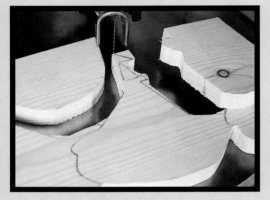

▲ Once the majority of the waste is removed you can return to the detailed areas

7 Sand all the cut edges with 150 grade abrasive paper and the face of the wood with 240 grade. Round over all the edges with the finer grade paper.

▲ The towel rail is ready for decorating

8 For the toilet roll holder, you will need to drill a hole through the dowel to accommodate the rope. Clamp the dowel in a vice or to a firm surface with waste wood under the dowel. Use the 10mm lip and spur drill bit on medium to high speed. Sand any tear out.

Remove the photocopy and lightly sand. With a soft pencil darken all these incised lines, this is part of the finished decoration.

10 Dilute small amounts of emulsion with plenty of water to produce a transparent wash, which will colour the wood without obscuring the grain. Paint each adjacent area different colours keeping to a palette of five colours. Let each colour dry before painting in the area adjoining it, to avoid runs. Paint each knob the same colour as the

6 The maximum area of waste is removed with a single line of sawing. Each inside corner should be sawn into from one side, the blade backed up and the sawing line carried on, as explained in step 3. Remove the waste at inside corners, and around vulnerable areas like the pennant flag being careful not to flex the wood.

9 Trace over the design with a bradawl or other sharp point to incise the design into the wood underneath your photocopy.

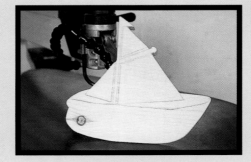

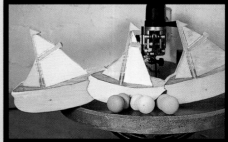

▲ The decorated towel rail ready for assembly

◄ The design is transferred to the wood

hulls of the boat, so that they blend in when assembled. Paint the dowel for the toilet roll holder.

11 When the paint is dry apply two coats of quick drying clear matt varnish. This varnish dries in two hours, has no odour and brushes can be washed out in water.

▲ Finishing the work with matt varnish

12 To hang both pieces, attach mirror plates to the back of the work, by drilling two sizes of blind hole - the hole is not visible at the front of the work - that slightly overlap, one above the other, thus creating the keyhole effect that secures the item to the wall mounted screw. The size of drill bits needed will depend on the mirror plate chosen.

14 Thread the rope through the dowel and knot to secure. Make a loop at the opposite end, adjusting the length to suit. Thread with the rolls of tissue paper and slip the loop over the knob and tighten.

13 Use the 2mm drill bit to make pilot holes for attaching the knobs, which are then screwed on.

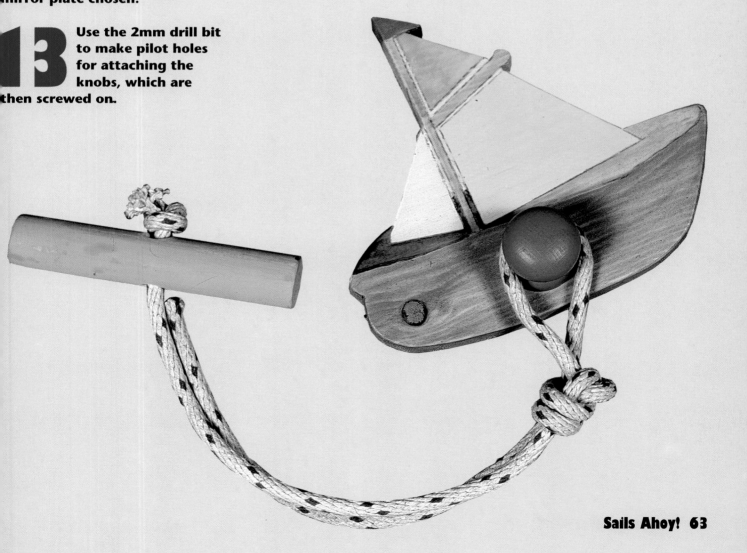

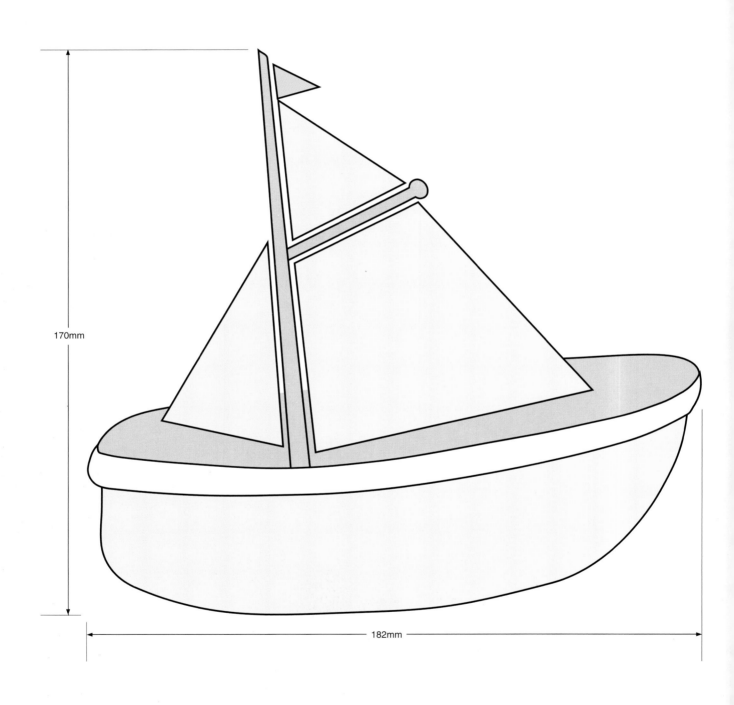

170mm

182mm

Thomas comes home!

With a three-year-old grandson, obsessed by Thomas the Tank Engine **Jack Marsh** makes his day

When my grandson needed a couple of coat hooks in his bedroom his mother suggested that they be made in the form of an engine wall plaque to provide some decorative interest. Here is the resulting design, with projecting buffers accommodating the hanging loops on the dressing gown.

All the engines in the 'Thomas' series have faces on the smoke box doors but it was decided to omit this feature so that, hopefully, it would not be outgrown quite so soon.

Method

The construction is very simple and is known as appliqué or overlay technique; it entails starting with the largest (cab) piece and successively gluing the remaining pieces on top of each other after shaping them. This complete assembly is then backed with a piece of 4mm (5/32in) ply so that a wall fixing can be made through the cab windows. Rather than counter sink into this thin material it's best to use screw cups which, if left to show look rather like eyes. I elected to cover the screw heads with circular pieces of veneer, cut with scissors and held in with Blu-Tack to facilitate subsequent removal. Let the backing ply project about 25mm (1in) below the cab back so that the wheel silhouettes can be worked in it.

To enhance the 3D effect of the plaque I used contrasting woods with the darkest at the back (rosewood) and the lightest at the front (beech) with the middle section of iroko. Combinations of other timbers would be just as effective.

1 Make paper patterns for the cab, the funnel and the mid-boiler section and ensure these are symmetrical by cutting them from folded paper (see Patterns, Fig 1). The smoke box, being circular, can be marked directly on to the wood with a pair of compasses.

2 Cut out all the major pieces with the scrollsaw and finish by sanding the edges, some of which will

▲ An improvised sanding table

▼ Producing true circular forms with a sanding disc

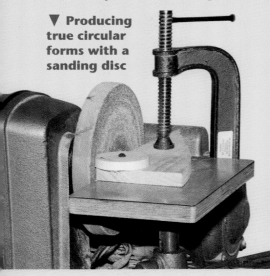

▲ Bevelling the face of a disc for the smoke-box. Note the guide block to maintain the bevel angle

need to be well rounded over. For this a powered sanding disc is invaluable so it is worth digressing to examine some possible ways of achieving this.

Some readers will possess a special purpose sanding machine, others, like myself, may have a lathe to which a disc can easily be attached, with a sanding table, if needed, held in the toolrest support. Failing that, an electric drill can be held in a horizontal stand and a sanding table improvised by blocks of wood to provide work support at about centre height. If you don't possess a commercial horizontal stand it is very easy to make up a perfectly serviceable stand (shown in Patterns, Fig 2) which can be cramped to the bench.

3 A lathe was used to produce the buffers and also the smoke box and door detail to which the handle was added, made from a short length of 6mm (¼in) dowel and two bits of cocktail stick glued into holes in the dowel.

4 An alternative method of producing the circular components without a lathe is shown in the photograph. After scrollsawing them oversize, mount them to

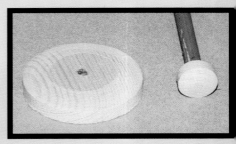

▲ Smoke box and buffer shaped by sanding disc. Another, thinner disc could indicate a door

overlap a flat piece of scrap using a snug-fitting round head screw. Cramp this set-up to the sanding table and rotate the wheel against the revolving disc to produce accurate circular discs. Tap the assembly closer and rotate again to reduce the diameter as required. The sanding disc can also be employed to form a bevel on the smoke box and buffers.

▲ Rounding off with the drill-driven disc

5 Securely mount the component on a length of dowel and again rotate it against the revolving disc but this time in a vertical position. The guide block cramped to the table top helps to maintain a consistent bevel angle. Make sure there is adequate clearance between the sanding disc and table so that the work can't be trapped between them.

6 Funnel

The base of the funnel is notched so that it can be glued to

▶ The two-piece funnel construction

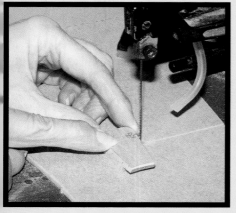

▲ The joint on the funnel being cut to accept the ring piece. Note: the hardboard ancillary table to provide close lower support when cutting small pieces

▲ The funnel ring. For ease of handling cut all details before parting off

the middle (boiler) section and it will need further tailoring with a chisel to accommodate the rounded edge of the smoke box to which it also abuts.

The ring around the top of the funnel is made by jointing in a separate piece before any rounding is carried out.

7 Cab Roof

This was a thin 1.5mm (¹⁄₁₆in) strip of hardwood cut to overhang the can at the front and both sides but flush at the back. It was fixed in place with glue and stainless steel escutcheon pins positioned every 6mm (¼in). These pins have prominent domed heads and are intended to represent rivets. There is a danger of splitting the cab back when driving so many close pins into a thin dense timber so it's best to pre-drill. If you lack the right sized bit, nip the head off one of the pins and use that as a drill. This works like a bradawl and forms a hole by compressing the fibres aside.

8 Drill holes in the buffer bar to accept the buffers and then apply a clear finish to all components before assembly, avoiding those surfaces which will subsequently receive glue.

Glue all components together in correct sequence and finally add plywood backing. This can be glued on slightly oversize and trimmed flush afterwards with the scrollsaw, at the same time the wheels can be indicated in silhouette form.

▲ After shaping, the funnel is glued to the mid-boiler section. Leave the edge square at the joint

▼ The veneer 'plugs' in the cab windows are held with Blu-Tack

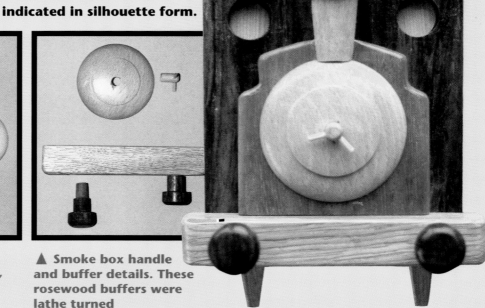

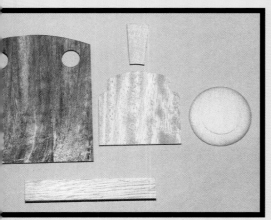

▲ The major components cut out. Some will need further edge shaping, but preserve a square edge where funnel joins the 'boiler'

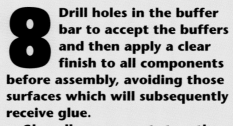

▲ Smoke box handle and buffer details. These rosewood buffers were lathe turned

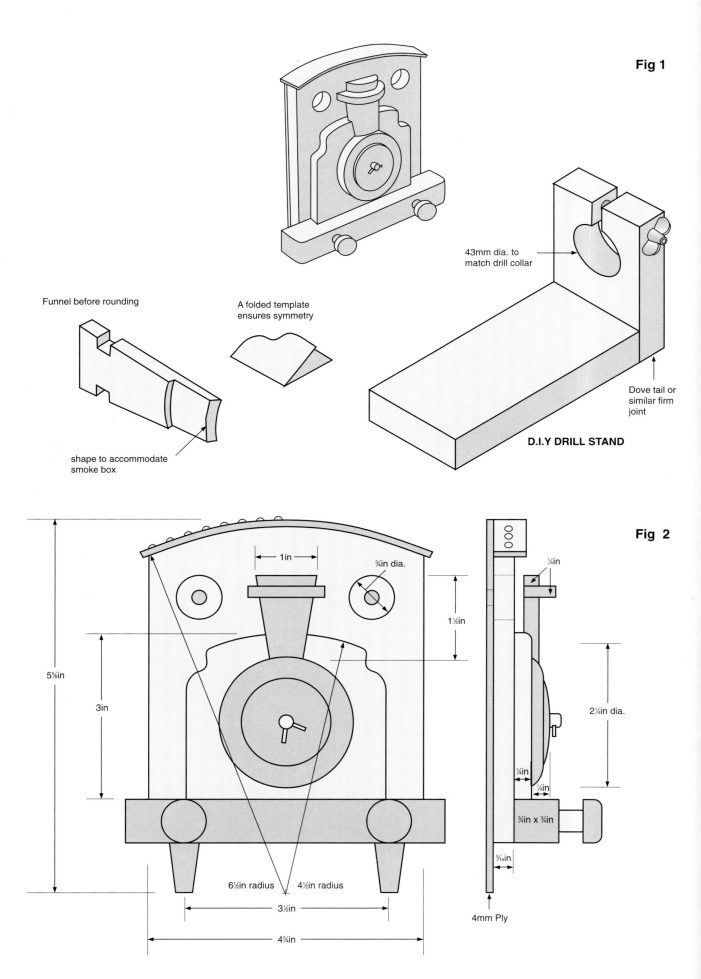

Fig 1

Funnel before rounding

A folded template
ensures symmetry

43mm dia. to
match drill collar

shape to accommodate
smoke box

Dove tail or
similar firm
joint

D.I.Y DRILL STAND

Fig 2

1in

¾in dia.

¼in

1½in

5⅝in

3in

2¼in dia.

¼in

¼in

¾in x ¾in

6½in radius

4½in radius

3½in

4¾in

⅝in

4mm Ply

Sails Ahoy! Part II

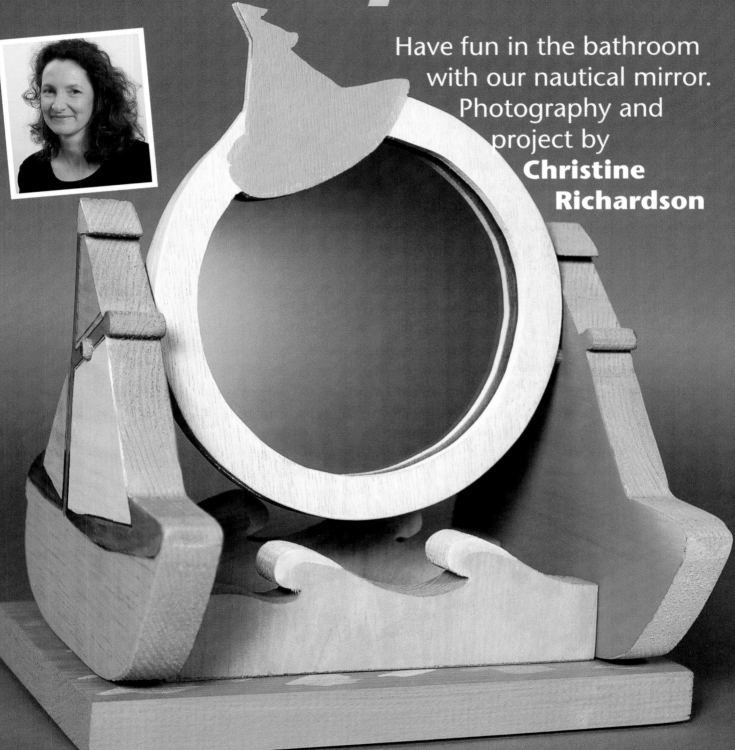

Have fun in the bathroom with our nautical mirror. Photography and project by **Christine Richardson**

This bathroom mirror completes our three-piece bathroom set that we began earlier in the book. Although there may be some techniques here that you have not tried before, there is a natural progression from the first two items so do have a go. If you find any problems please write to us and let us know, or when you make the project why not send us a picture? For this project it is helpful, but not essential, to have access to a workbench, woodworkers vice and an electric palm sander in addition to the following tools and materials. If you would like to order a back issue, with plans and instructions for the rest of this set, please turn to the front of the magazine for information.

▲ Lay your templates on your timber

1 Photocopy the templates from the centre pages of this issue twice. Cut around the outline and stick to your timber with repositionable Spraymount. Alternatively transfer the outline by drawing around the template, in which case you need only one photocopy.

▲ Separate each piece before sawing the outline

2 Cut out each boat roughly so that they are on separate pieces of wood. Saw along the outline of the bottom of the boats and then continue to the sails and masts. As you approach inside corners, continue the cutting line into the corner, back the blade up a couple of millimetres into the line just sawn and gradually realign to a less acute angle, this may mean allowing the blade to nibble the wood, while you turn the timber gradually without pushing it onto the blade. Carry on the cut and regain the line after the corner.

3 When the majority of waste has been removed, return to the small amount of waste left at inside corners and approach it

▲ Remove the waste from inside corners with a second cut

from the opposite side cutting along the line to meet the first cut in the corner. If the corner seems too acute, make a central saw cut straight to the corner and then make two more cuts along the outline from opposite directions, to remove the waste area on each side.

4 Still using the straight blade cut a piece of the pine 23cm long using the full width of the plank. This is the base for the stand.

Cutting list

- 14cm diameter mirror glass
- 1m @ 170 x 20mm prepared pine
- 20 x 60cm @ 3mm oak-faced plywood

Materials

- 15mm veneer pins
- 2 x 8mm fluted dowels
- 240 and 150 grade abrasive paper
- Variety of emulsion test pots
- Quick-drying clear matt varnish

Tools

- 22 tpi spiral blade
- 10 tpi blade for 25–50mm timber
- 2B pencil
- Bradawl
- 3mm and 8mm drill bits
- Compass (optional)
- Medium and fine craft paint brush

▲ Change blades to suit straight and curvy outlines

5 Before changing blades cut out the bottom edge of each of the 'waves'. Now change to the spiral blade, which is better suited to cutting out curves, and cut out the top edge of the 'waves'. These add stability to your mirror stand.

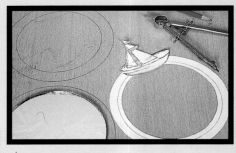

▲ Cut out three pieces of plywood for the mirror frame

6 Cut three 20cm squares of the plywood, each one will be a layer in your mirror frame. Stack the three pieces of plywood, good side up, and stick on or draw the largest circle, plus the small boat, on the top piece, remember to have grain running top to bottom.

Drill a hole for the saw blade ▲ to pass through

7 Using veneer pins, pin the pieces together on the outside of your cutting line. You are now going to saw through all three pieces together, this is called 'stack' sawing. Use the spiral

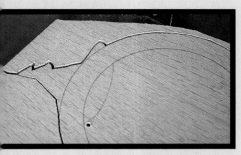

▲ Saw the outside outline of the mirror frames

blade and be careful to turn the work so that you are always pushing the blade backwards and not sideways. It is very easy to make this mistake as spiral blades will cut in any direction having teeth on all faces, not just the front leading edge.

▲ Saw the inside outline of the mirror frame

8 Once you have cut out your three circles, separate them into top, middle and bottom. The bottom piece is now ready. The middle piece has the centre removed to accommodate the mirror, so centre the mirror on the timber and draw around it, leaving equal amounts of frame at the edge. The top or

▲ The three mirror frames

front of the frame also has the centre removed but overlaps the edge of the mirror to hold it in place. Use the compass or the template to mark an inner circle which allows the frame to overlap the mirror by about 5mm.

9 Take the middle and front frames and with a 3mm drill bit make a hole next to the cutting line through which you can thread the saw blade.

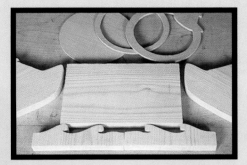

▲ Components ready for assembly

10 Release the tension on the scroll saw blade and remove it from the top clamp, raise the saw arm and thread the blade through the drill hole. Re-clamp the blade and re-tension. Saw out the waste from the centre and repeat for both the middle and front frames.

▲ Use veneer pins to assemble the mirror frame

11 Fit the mirror into the middle frame and sandwich between the back and front frames, check that the front

▲ Paint detail on the outside face of the boats and the rest plain blue

frame is veneer face outwards, stack them neatly and then use veneer pins to hold the three frames together, put them in from the back. Sand the inside edge of the front frame.

Finishing

12 Now that all your pieces are ready for finishing, sand all the cut edges with 150 grade abrasive paper and the face of the wood with 240 grade. Round over all the edges with the finer grade paper. Alternatively use an electric palm sander, which will speed up the process, leaving you only the inside edges to finish by hand.

13 Place the boat template on your work and trace the outline of the mast and sails with a bradawl or other sharp point to incise the design into the wood underneath your photocopy. With a soft pencil darken all these incised lines; this is part of the finished decoration.

14 Dilute small amounts of emulsion with plenty of water to produce a transparent wash, which will colour the wood without obscuring the grain. Paint each adjacent area of the boats

▲ Drill bits masked off for maximum drilling depth ensure the mirror is not broken when drilling the locating holes for the dowel

different colours keeping to a palette of 4 or 5 colours. Paint the mirror frame white and the small boat blue. Paint the inside face of the boats blue. The base is also blue with small white waves painted on. The cut-out waves are blue with the wave crests painted white. Let each colour dry before painting in the area adjoining it, to avoid runs.

Assembly

15 The mirror swivels on a pair of 8mm fluted dowels set 2cm below the central line. Drill a pilot hole for these with an 8mm lip and spur drill bit. Finish

▲ Drilling the holes for the dowel, note the waste wood under the work

Tip Measure the maximum depth that the drill bit can go without catching the edge of the mirror and mask it off. As you drill watch that the masking tape does not enter the hole and you will not drill too deeply.
   Always place a piece of waste wood underneath anything you are drilling to prevent damage to your work surface and the drill bit.

▲ Getting ready for final assembly

the hole which must not be more than 7mm deep, with a plain drill bit. It is best to use a vice for this procedure or get someone to hold it steady for you. Use quick-setting wood glue to fit the dowels into these holes and leave to fully cure over night. Remember to check that the dowels are horizontal, the best way is to lay the mirror on a ruler, laid at the level of the dowels and adjust them to a straight line.

16 Both boat-shaped stands need to be drilled to accept the other ends of the dowel. Drill an 8mm hole, completely through your timber, at the point marked on your template.

17 Draw the positions of the waves and the boats on the bottom of the base as a guide for screwing them in position. Use two No 8 countersunk woodscrews for each piece. Drill pilot holes first with a 3mm lip and spur or plain drill bit.

► The waves are attached

18 Attach the waves first by holding them securely against the base and slowly screwing them on.

▲ The mirror and boats ready for assembly

19 The boat side pieces are attached to either side of the mirror by gently twisting them on. The end of each dowel should be more or less flush with the outside face of each boat.

20 Screw the boats into position one at a time, squeezing them hard against the base board and the ends of the waves. If you wish you could also screw through the sides of the boats into the waves, but the construction is quite solid without this.

▲ The mirror stand is ready

21 Now that the mirror is assembled, apply two coats of quick-drying clear matt varnish to all sides. This varnish dries in two hours, has no odour and brushes can be washed out in water.

Attaching the mirror to the base ►

◄ Ready for varnishing

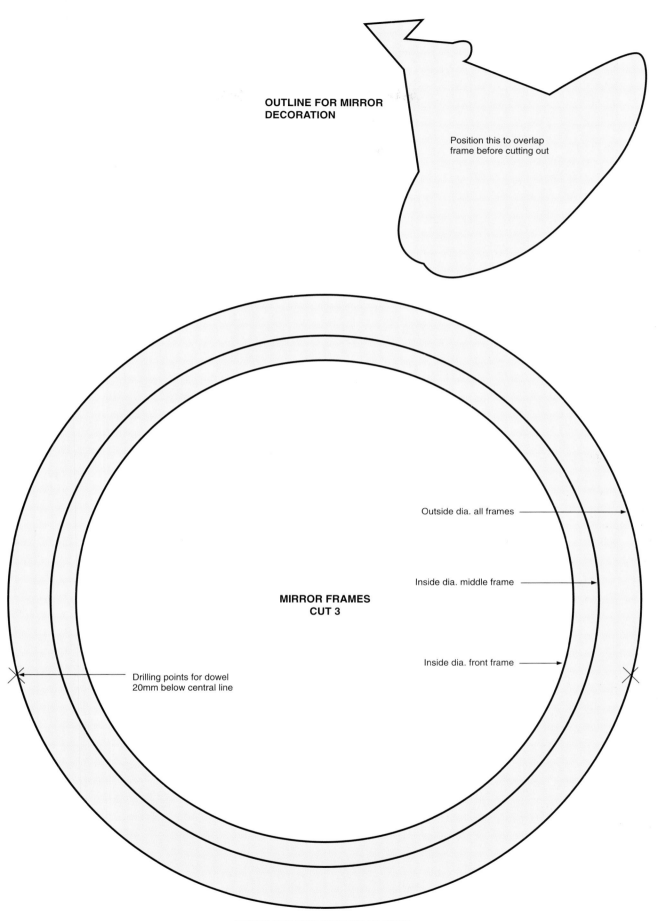

OUTLINE FOR MIRROR DECORATION

Position this to overlap frame before cutting out

Outside dia. all frames

Inside dia. middle frame

MIRROR FRAMES CUT 3

Inside dia. front frame

Drilling points for dowel 20mm below central line

TEMPLATE FOR MIRROR FRAMES

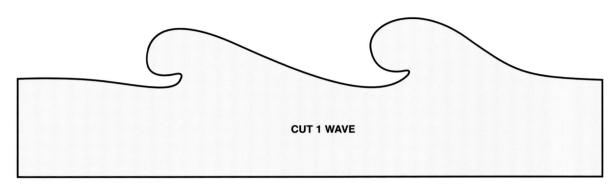

CUT 1 WAVE

TEMPLATE FOR WAVES

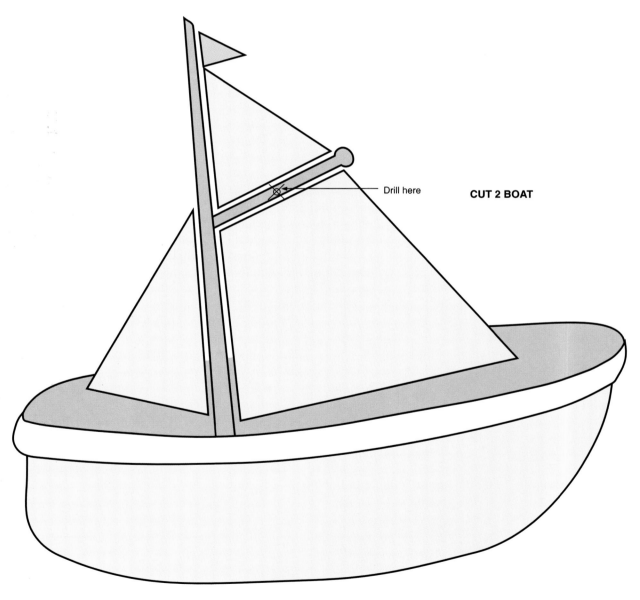

Drill here

CUT 2 BOAT

TEMPLATE FOR MIRROR STAND SHOWING DRILLING POINT FOR DOWEL

Celtic Christmas

Method

1 Cut about two dozen pieces of card big enough for the designs, together with two pieces of 4mm plywood as backings.

2 Using PVA glue, stick the drawn designs to the top piece of plywood and place on top of a stack of card with the second piece of plywood as the bottom, like a sandwich!

3 The stack is nailed through all thicknesses using 25mm panel pins. To prevent the nails penetrating the workbench, I place the stack on a piece of 12mm steel plate recycled from my local scrap merchant. This process of pinning keeps all the card together as solid as a piece of wood. ▼

4 The next step is to drill pilot holes 1.5mm in all the areas to be pierced. After drilling, the blade can be introduced to the internal areas and the piercing done. ▼

John Burke says you need never panic about Christmas cards again

Well, I don't know about you, but every year I panic about Christmas cards, but no more!

In each of the 15 years that I've been making my own, I've always meant to start earlier, and ended up with the area around my scrollsaw looking like Santa's Workshop, with bits of cut-out festive decorations and baubles.

In the past I've cut out Christmas trees, angels, snow flakes, carol singers and almost every symbol associated with the festive season. This year I'm trying a non-denominational design, including my interest in Celtic knotwork into the design by working around the theme of 'Noel' and using a knot or two as decoration.

First choose your lettering, perhaps after consulting one of the plentiful calligraphy pattern books, which are full of ideas.

The knot design, however, is more specialised, and my source book was Sheila Sturrock's *Celtic Knotwork Designs*.

With the designs chosen, the next matter to be decided is the card's format. Previously I have used all colours of backing, but this time I went for combinations like black with white lettering and white card with red and green, experimenting until I found the one I liked best.

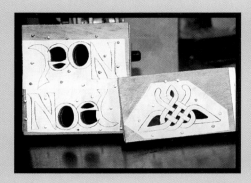

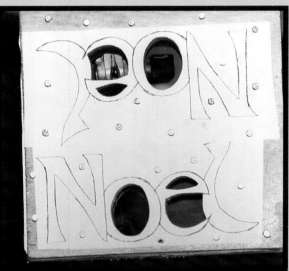

5 Several blades of 32 tpi will be used during the piercing as paper and card are quite abrasive — due to the inclusion of china clay in their production — and the blades blunt quite quickly. After piercing, the outer profile can be cut and the individual layers separated. ▼

"I've always meant to start earlier, and ended up with the area around my scrollsaw looking like Santa's Workshop, with bits of cut-out festive decorations and baubles"

6 Shadow lines between the letters of the 'Noel' can be done with a felt-tip pen. ▼

7 Highlight detail ▶ is added with a silver pen.

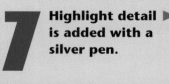

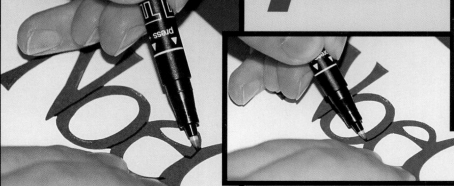

8 The silver pen is used to fill ▶ in the crossover interlaced portions of the Celtic knots.

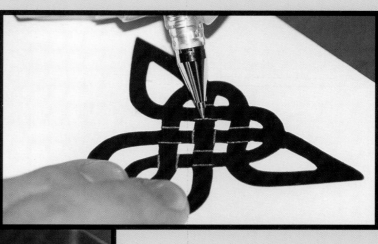

9 Assemble the cut-outs on the backing card, making the job much easier by using a credit card to apply the glue in a thin layer to a piece of perspex. ▼

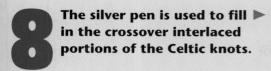

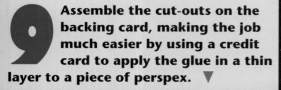

10 Drop each cut-out in turn onto the glue.

11 With the help of a fine ▲ pair of tweezers pick up each cut-out in turn and place in position.

12 When I had finished I had four prototypes with different colour combinations and arrangements, my favourite being the black card with red 'Noel' and green knots.

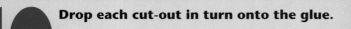

Celtic Knotwork Designs is published by GMC Publications Ltd, ISBN 1 86108 040 9, and available mail order from Guild of Master Craftsman Publications Ltd, Castle Place, 167 High Street, Lewes, East Sussex BN7 1XU, credit card hotline 01273 488005, fax 01273 478606.

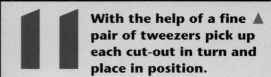

Flower Bower

A pair of plant holders for the windowsill and wall, make the most of the tilt facility on your scrollsaw table

Project and photography by **Christine Richardson**

These designs are easily adapted to fit your own requirements, just repeat the design. For planting directly into them, buy a length of absorbent hanging basket liner or use them simply as covers for plastic windowboxes. Add drainage holes for outside use or use a saucer under house plants to catch the drips.

Wall hanging window box

1 Photocopy the template for the front of the window box. Either cut out the design or stick it to the timber with Spraymount so that it is easily removed later. There are five pieces to each of these projects, both ends of the base and side pieces are angled, this angle is determined by the diagonal sides of the front and back pieces.

▲ Saw the diagonal sides of the front and back pieces

2 Use the 10 tpi straight blade to cut the diagonal sides of both the back and front.

▲ Adjust the tilt of the table until the diagonal edge is parallel with the blade

3 Adjust the tilting table so that the diagonal side of either a front or back piece is vertical and parallel to the blade while the

base is flat on the table. This is the angle of cut for the other pieces.

4 Cut the base with the ends angled in opposite directions and the side pieces with both ends angled in one direction.

5 Take the front piece with the design on, and drill a small pilot hole in each of the closed areas of the design.

Materials

- 3m length of planed pine 15 x 145cm finished size
- 2.5cm (1in) panel pins or electric pinning gun
- Quick-setting wood glue
- Emulsion paint
- Exterior varnish

Tools

- Scrollsaw
- 10 tpi blades for straight lines
- 20 tpi spiral blades for curvy lines
- 240 grade abrasive paper
- Hammer or electric pinning gun
- Lip and spur wood drills
- Household paint brush

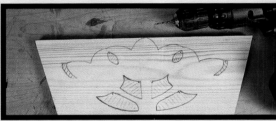

▲ Cut the angled ends of both sides and the base

◄ The five pieces of the project, before the design is sawn

Drill a pilot hole for the saw blade in each of the closed areas of the design ▼

6 Using the spiral saw blade for the design, release the tension on the blade and release the blade from the top clamp and thread it through the pilot hole in the timber, re-clamp in the upper clamp and re-tension. Remove the waste wood and repeat for each area of the fretted design.

▲ Sawing the fretted design

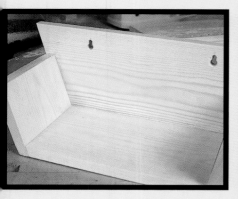

▲ Make the key hole slots for wall mounting before you assemble the box

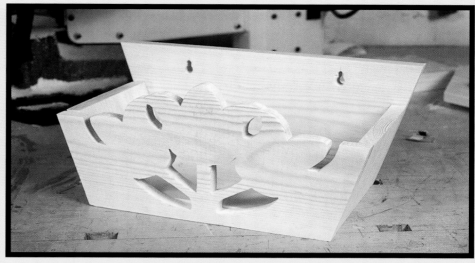

▲ The project before finishing

7 To make the key holes for wall mounting, divide the length of the window box by three and mark two crosses for the first holes. Take two different sized wood drills and use the larger one to make the first hole. Make another pair of crosses directly above the first and drill here with the smaller drill. Neaten any tear out.

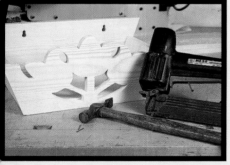

▲ Use panel pins and a hammer or an electric pinning gun

8 Sand the whole piece before assembly. To assemble, stand the base on one long edge, arrange the two end pieces so that they are stood at either side of the base with bottom edges level. Glue lightly along the uppermost edges. Take the back piece and position carefully, trying not to move the pieces underneath. When you are satisfied that everything is in position use the panel pins or pinning gun to secure.

9 Turn over the work so that the back is flat on the workbench and glue the uppermost edges. Position the front and secure as before. Drill five drainage holes in the base if you plan to use this box outdoors.

Windowsill box

1 Copy steps 1–3 given in wall hanging box.

2 Take the front and back pieces and saw down both sides of each of the three arched shapes, this helps you to complete a cut without having to back the

▲ Make relief cuts on either side of the arched shapes

blade out. By meeting the bottom of the pre-cut shape the blade is released when it meets the corner instead of being trapped.

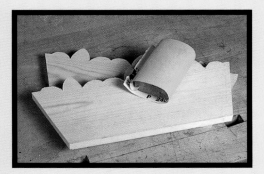

▲ Sand all parts thoroughly before assembly

3 Sand all pieces very thoroughly before assembly.

4 Assemble the box as steps 7–8 above, except that this time the side pieces are placed with the top edges level, so that about half a centimetre is left protruding at the bottom to form feet which raise the box off the ground.

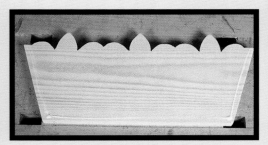

▲ Glue shows position of base and sides for assembly

▲ One last piece to secure with glue on uppermost edge

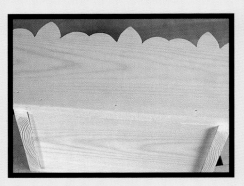

▲ Ready for pinning

Finishing

The projects were finished with ordinary matt emulsion paint greatly thinned with water to retain the grain pattern, and then given several coats of matt varnish. This approach gives a wide choice of colour and a small test pot would be enough for several window boxes. As the paint is very liquid, wipe over the freshly painted surface with kitchen paper to prevent runs

▼ Both planters with paint finish and leave

Tips

Spiral blades cut curvy profiles more easily than straight blades and make tight corners easier too. Because the blade cuts a line or 'kerf' that is as wide as the blade at any angle, the work is easily turned to cut difficult outlines and tight inside corners.

Using thinner timber for this project or a chunkier blade would have meant that identically paired parts of these projects could have been pinned together and sawn at the same time, with a time saving method called 'stack sawing'. Never force the blade to cut through thicker timber than it can easily cope with, the likelihood is that the blade will snap and even if it doesn't the results will be very poor.

to dry. If the colour is too pale apply a second coat.

Alternatively, there are a variety of pleasantly coloured wood preservatives available for interior and exterior use, and although they are more expensive they do offer colour and preservative treatment in one product.

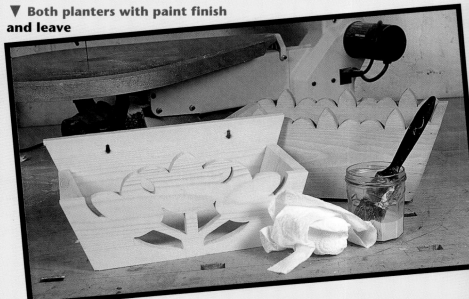

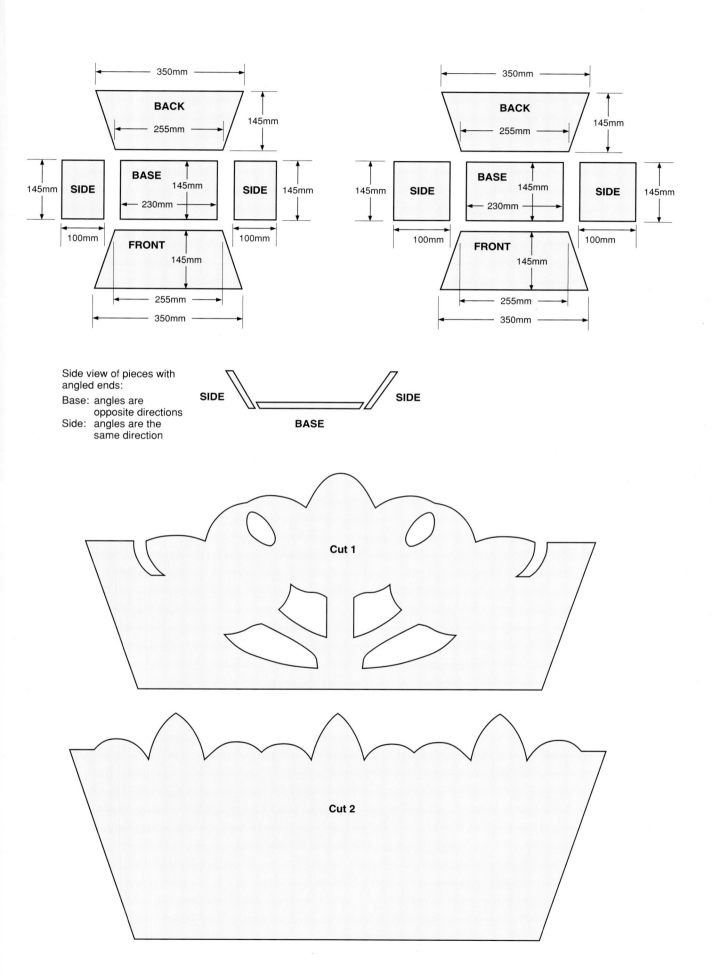

350mm

BACK

255mm

145mm

145mm SIDE BASE 145mm SIDE 145mm

230mm

100mm 100mm

FRONT

145mm

255mm

350mm

350mm

BACK

255mm

145mm

145mm SIDE BASE 145mm SIDE 145mm

230mm

100mm 100mm

FRONT

145mm

255mm

350mm

Side view of pieces with angled ends:

Base: angles are opposite directions
Side: angles are the same direction

SIDE   SIDE

BASE

Cut 1

Cut 2

All shuttered up

A traditional folk design adorns these practical and charming window shutters Project and Photography by **Christine Richardson**

Add detail to a small window with these useful shutters. The fretwork design is based on the dove and heart, traditionally symbols of peace and love, perfect for a bedroom. The timber is birch ply, which unlike solid wood won't warp and twist with the changing seasons, and gives a high quality finish suitable for clear varnish or painting if you prefer. Although this is not a difficult scrollsaw project and the shutters themselves are easy to make, fitting them can be time consuming and may require specialist tools like a block plane. A cordless screwdriver would be a great help, too; in my example – for a very small window – there are no less than 44 screws in each shutter. Please note that the instructions here are for shutters fitted inside the window reveal.

1 Measure your window opening height and width in at least two different places to find the maximum measurement.

2 Divide the width of the opening by four for the two pairs of shutters. The second shutter in each pair is made 15mm narrower, so that when the shutters are in their open position folded back against the wall, the outside edge butts neatly against the added 12mm strip of pine and does not overlap it. To achieve this fit, add 7.5mm to the width of the first shutter in the pair and subtract 7.5mm from the width of the second shutter, i.e. window opening total width 970mm.

970 ÷ 4 = 242.5mm
242.5 + 7.5 = 250mm
(first shutter)
242.5 - 7.5 = 235mm
(second shutter)

You will need to cut two shutters at each of these widths, the lengths of course will be identical. For example the cutting list for the plywood in our project was:
2 @ 840 x 250 x 12mm
2 @ 840 x 235 x 12mm

3 Make the measurements before ordering your timber and ask the timber merchant to cut it to size for you. If you intend to finish the shutters with clear varnish, ask them to cut the plywood with the grain running lengthwise.

4 If your window opening is very irregular in shape follow the directions below for fitting the shutters before you scroll saw your design, otherwise you risk having a design which is off-centre once fitted.

5 Use the template centrally in the top third of the shutter. Either photocopy the design and stick it onto the timber or simply draw around it. The design is arranged so that the

Materials

- Birch faced plywood to fit your window opening
- 2 @ 12 x 12mm pine the height of your window opening
- 2 lengths of piano hinge
- 6 @ 65mm butt hinges
- 10mm wood screws size 4 for piano hinges
- 16mm wood screws size 6 for butt hinges
- Quick-setting wood glue
- 20mm panel pins

Tools

- 22 tpi spiral blade
- Philips screwdriver
- 2mm drill bit and drill
- Steel tape measure

▲ Draw the design onto the shutter

birds face each other at the central hinge on each shutter.

6 Drill a pilot hole through each part of the closed design near to an edge or corner.

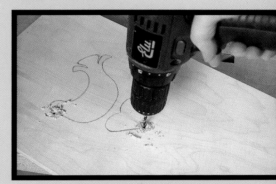

▲ Drill pilot holes inside the closed design

▲ Thread the blade through the pilot holes

7 Clamp the blade in the lower clamp and thread it through the pilot hole, then secure in the upper clamp. Tension the blade.

8 Cut out the design. Release the tension on the blade and remove the blade from the upper clamp. Take the work off the

Attaching the hinges

▲ Cut out the closed design

One pair of shutters with the birds facing the central join

table and re-thread the blade through the next pilot hole. Secure the blade in the top clamp, re-tension and continue to saw out the design. Check that your design is kept in pairs so that the birds face each other. To ensure that the design is placed in the same position on each subsequent shutter, lay the first shutter on top and make registration marks through the cut out design. Use these registration marks to position the original template and then draw the design on the next shutter, this will ensure that each bird is in the same place and the same size.

10 Lay each pair of shutters right side up, this is the side that faces into the room. Mark this side with a pencil, 'A' and 'B'. Turn the pair over, closely butted together and lay the piano hinge down the centre join, being careful to ensure it is truly central.

▲ A cordless screwdriver is useful where so many screws are involved

bounce when the hinge is closed, the hinge will need to be moved. Unscrew one side of the hinge completely, leaving it attached to one shutter and check that the screw holes line up with the previously drilled holes, if not mark the holes again, drill new pilot holes and screw the hinge in the new alignment, this should cure the problem.

▲ Position the piano hinge and drill pilot holes

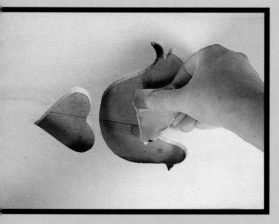

▲ Sand the edges of the design

9 When all the designs are cut, sand the edges.

11 Mark through each screw hole in the hinge with a pencil and then drill pilot holes for the screws, being careful not to drill right through to the front.

12 Screw the piano hinge in position and check that the two halves will lay flat to one another, if there is any

13 Keep the shutters face down and fully open on the worktop. On the lengthwise edge of the wider shutter, lay a line of glue.

▼ Glue down the long edge of the larger shutter

▲ Use panel pins to hold the wood in place until the glue sets

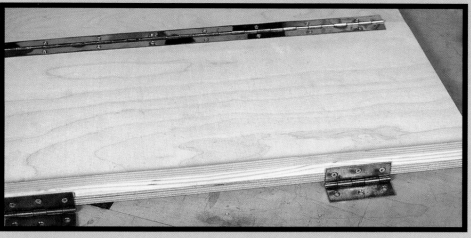

▲ Position the butt hinges on the strengthened edge, lined up with the front edge of the shutter

14 Take the 12mm x 12mm length of pine and lay it along this glued edge. Use panel pins to hold it until the glue dries.

15 Attach three butt hinges down this strengthened edge. First attach the top and bottom hinge, about 100mm from the end of the edge, then centre the last hinge between the two. Mark the place for the pilot holes through

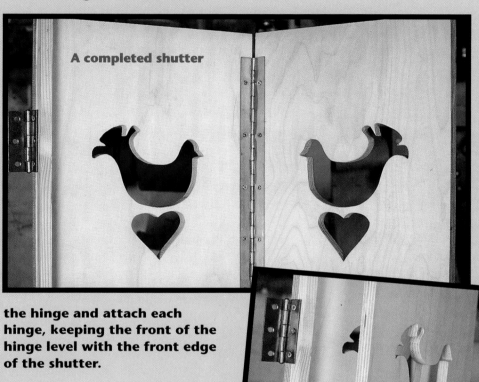

A completed shutter

the hinge and attach each hinge, keeping the front of the hinge level with the front edge of the shutter.

Fitting the shutters

16 Hold the shutter to the window frame and check for a good fit. If there is any need to trim the shutters, mark the areas that need trimming with a pencil and trim with the scroll saw or a block plane.

17 Once each pair of shutters is fitted and hung, check for fit at the centre, if there is any overlap here, divide it

▲ The smaller shutter fits neatly next to the pine strip when they are folded open

between the two shutters and trim as before.

18 When the shutters are hung and trimmed, they can be painted or varnished to finish.

Tips

- Steel hinges, while inexpensive, will need painting, so remember to use a metal primer first. Brass hinges should be fitted and then masked off before the shutters are painted to keep them clean.

- Cut the piano hinge with a hacksaw and file the cut edge to remove burrs.

- To keep the shutters closed, fix magnetic catches behind the bi-fold onto the windowsill.

- To keep the shutters open and flat against the wall, use small hasp and staple or cupboard latches fixed to the wall.

SHUTTERS TEMPLATE
(ACTUAL SIZE)

A cut above the rest

A utilitarian object can also be beautiful as **Jack Hudson** demonstrates here with three-colour chopping boards

Y ou can follow the principles of bevel cutting or intarsia work for these boards, well-known by scrollsawers, or you can keep it simple.

There are a number of options open to you. The use of three different woods for colour and contrast makes this chopping board a most attractive addition to the kitchen, as shown in the illustrations here.

If you only make one chopping board and use bevel cutting there will be a lot of cutting to waste. If you make two boards and use vertical cuts with the scrollsaw you will have very little waste.

Design

This is a sensible size of board and was determined by consulting the chef de cuisine. It needs to be large enough so that chopped pieces do not drift off on to the working top and also to accommodate long stems like celery. Make it smaller if you wish.

Obviously there are numerous patterns that you can adopt, the simplest being alternating stripes or a chequerboard of different woods, but these do not display your skill with the scrollsaw.

Two designs are shown here. The first is the Oriental Yin and Yang pattern (see Fig 1 in Patterns) and is the one illustrated in the colour pictures. An alternative using a

mock jigsaw puzzle pattern (see Fig 2) is also attractive and only uses two colours so that it is more economical in wood.

The beauty of these boards comes from the use of attractive timbers in close relationship with each other. It is not really practical to use colour finishes or stains for a chopping board because knives will etch into the surface during years of use.

Obtaining a pleasing contrast calls for a white wood, a dark red and a gold or brown. The most suitable white woods are beech, maple and sycamore. Dark red timbers might be chosen from any of the mahogany family such as meranti, utile or sapele. The third colour could be a brown such as walnut or a golden colour such as spruce, or larch. The woods illustrated here are sycamore, African mahogany and larch.

The best way to select the timber is go to a good timber yard and see what they have to offer. I am fortunate in having a really good timber man in Steve Collett at Cornish Woodcraft. He had some beautiful figured larch sheets because of a boat-building project he was engaged upon and so I chose that for my third colour.

By going to a real timber supplier you can select your woods and get an expert to machine them all to exactly the same thickness, and this will reduce the amount of cleaning up to do later.

Method

The board shown is made with vertical cuts on the scrollsaw. That is to say the blade is in the normal right angle position to the cutting table. It will be found that for a kitchen utensil this is quite satisfactory and a little judicious cleaning up by hand or with a drum or flap sander is more than adequate to give a good close fit.

Scrollsaws generally have a 50mm (2in) depth of cut and a 400mm (16in) throat which is well within the capacity required for this work.

1 Take a piece of sycamore and a piece of mahogany approximately 300mm (12in) square x 15mm (⅝in) thick and fix them together. Either use double sided tape or wood screws.

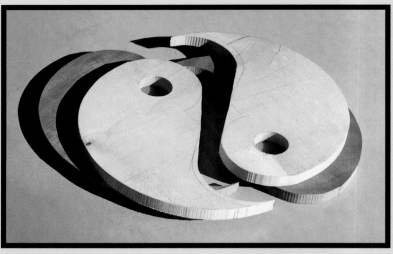

◄ After cutting out, the pieces are separated

2 Find the centre of the square boards from the intersection of the diagonals and draw a 140mm (5½in) radius circle. On the diameter, draw two part circles of 55mm (2¼in) radius and connect them with a tangent through the centre of the large circle. The centres of these two circles are also the centres for the 40mm (1⅝in) diameter holes. (See Fig 1, Patterns and photograph.)

3 Use an 8 tpi to 10 tpi blade in the scrollsaw to cut out the pieces. Do not hurry this part of the work, the more slowly and carefully the outline is followed,

the less cleaning and fitting work to be done later.

4 If the two pieces are cut together a hole will have to be drilled for the saw blade to cut out the 40mm (1⅝in) holes. In one of his projects, Patrick Spielman reduced the point of the blade to make the drill hole as inconspicuous as possible and this is one solution. An alternative is to separate the pieces after cutting out the main shapes and tackle the small holes separately. From the waste corner pieces, cut the 40mm (1³/8in) diameter discs and cut out the four holes separately. The waste from these internal holes will be discarded and so the drill hole for the saw blade is no longer a problem. An easier alternative if you have a large Forstner or expanding drill bit in

Two squares of contrasting woods are fixed together and marked before cutting out ►

▲ The central motif for one board

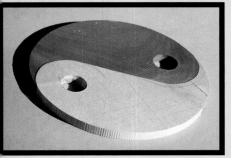

▲ The pieces for central motif fitted together and drilled

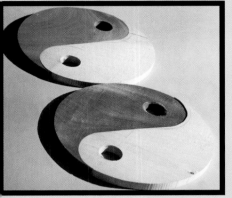

▲ Two boards for the price of one

a drill press is to drill the holes out and fit the discs into them.

5 After cutting out the main shapes and preparing the 40mm (1⁵/₈in) discs you have the basis for two boards.

6 To square the ends, two pieces of the third colour wood are cut to fit exactly round the large central motif. They are cut from 385mm (15³/₈in) long by 285mm (11¼in) wide pieces, and in the illustrations larch is used.

The central motif is framed in larch and the edge framing prepared and biscuit jointed ready for gluing ▼

7 Clean up all round and glue the pieces together. Trim the edges carefully with the plane ready to accept the framing.

8 Prepare the outside framing from 20mm x 15mm (¾in x ⁵/₈in) red wood.

9 The framing may be mitred round the glued-up board or biscuit-jointed into the edges.

10 Plane all the edges and round the corners of the boards. Smooth or round all edges with a small plane or sandpaper block. The board surface has to be cleaned smooth. It may need planing or better still scraping with a cabinet scraper before sanding.

Finishing

A chopping board will often be used in wet conditions and I always use Aerolite 306 two-part adhesive for strength and moisture resistance. The glue powder is mixed with a little water in a jar and will keep in a cool workshop for days. The acid hardener is applied to one face of the joint and the glue to the other and when the parts are clamped together they interact to form a very strong waterproof joint. It is also a good filling glue and will take up minor gaps. Cascamite is another synthetic resin and is a good waterproof filling adhesive, but after adding water to the powder it has to be used at once and this means having to throw away unused portions.

I must confess to a simple trick which I have used for years on turned and cabinet work. Save the very finest sawdust from the timber you are using and collect different wood dusts in plastic bags. When there is a gap, a crack or worm hole to fill, pack the hole with dry sawdust and then add a few drops of the thin penetrating cyanoacrylate glue and as it soaks in, top up the gap with dry dust. In a few seconds you have a perfectly filled gap with wood of the same colour as you are working. You must use the instant thin superglue for penetration. This can be sanded back to blend invisibly into the surface of the work. It will be found that the glue tends to darken as it sets into the dust and I usually use a lighter colour for this reason. This saves money on commercial woodfillers as well!

The final finish to use for work of this type is Rustin's teak oil. Apply the oil generously with a brush or rag and leave for five minutes to soak in. Then rub off the surplus with a cloth and put aside to dry overnight. Additional coats may be given, depending on the absorbency of the timber. Added coats may build up a gloss and if this is undesirable cut the shine back with 0000 wire wool. After weeks of use if the board needs freshening it is easy to give it another wipe of teak oil.

Suppliers

Axminster Power Tool Centre,
Chard Street,
Axminster, Devon. EX13 5DZ.
Tel: 01297-33656

Boddy's,
Boroughbridge,
North Yorkshire. YO5 9LJ.
Tel: 01423-322370

Craft Supplies Ltd.,
Miller's Dale, Buxton,
Derbyshire.SK17 8SN.
Tel: 01298-871636

Hobbies (Dereham) Ltd.,
Dereham,
Norfolk. NR19 2QZ.
Tel:01362-692985

W. Hobby Ltd.,
Knight's Hill Square,
London. SE27 0HH.
Tel: 0208-7614244

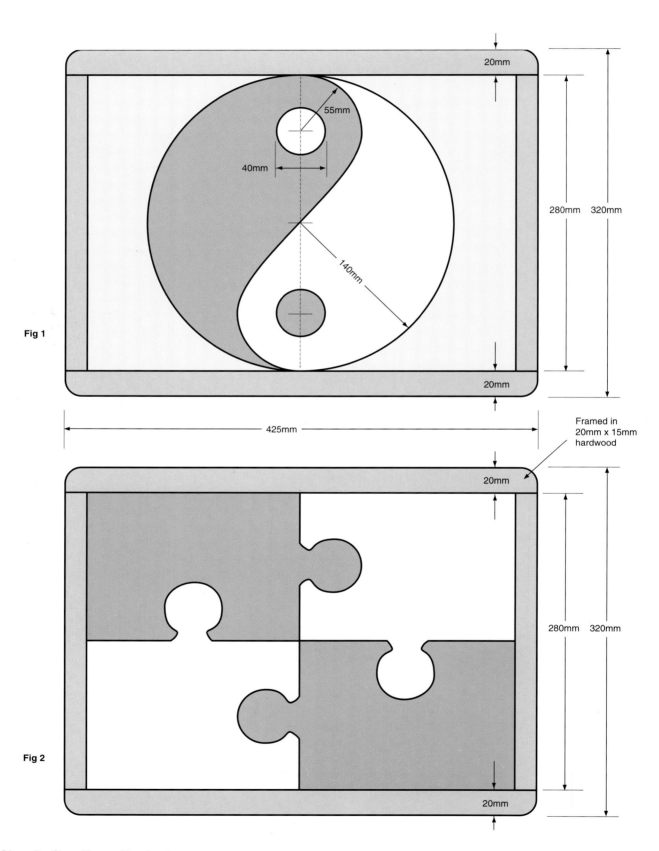

Fig 1

55mm

40mm

140mm

20mm

20mm

280mm

320mm

425mm

Framed in
20mm x 15mm
hardwood

Fig 2

20mm

20mm

280mm

320mm

Down on the Farm

A play farm designed by **Jack Hudson** for the enjoyment of children of any age that can be added to over a long period of time

This project shows you how to make a charming farmyard and country barn in which your children or grandchildren can store their farm animals and enjoy for many years to come. Perhaps you might like to add to it, too, with further outbuildings. Although this toy is based upon actual farmyards it must be emphasised that the object here is to make sturdy playthings for the younger child rather than a perfect model. The farmyard is not simply for display and to be looked at, it is for play. The scale also works with the superb range of authentic farm animals, tractors and other implements available in toy shops.

Design

Because this is a play farm, complications like Georgian windows and doors that open are not shown. There is no reason why enthusiastic model makers should not build upon these basic designs to produce realistic scale models. The universally accepted scale for doll's houses is 1/12th full size, but this is too large for model villages, railways or a farm layout and so the scale of 1/24th has been adopted. This is also a universal standard scale and there are specialist suppliers who cater for it. If you wish, you could obtain realistic little doors, windows and textured finishes for walls and roofs to suit the models (*see the Suppliers List*). Skilled miniaturists might

like to make their own animals, people and farm machinery, but for a toy it is much easier to buy them from a toy shop. The range made by BRITAINS is incredibly realistic, and although they are 1/32nd full size; this is a small difference and the designs presented here work well with them.

The Baseboard Large Board

This is a big toy and a busy parent will want to have something that can be stowed away easily after play. If all the farm buildings stand on the board it has to be 1500mm x 1000mm (59in x 39in). It is

Medium-sized farmyard board with Big Barn

made from 9mm ($^3/_8$in) MDF/plywood so that when placed on the floor it is strong enough for children to step on.

It is quite heavy and, on the pattern, I suggest that you might like to cut six large jigsaw pieces, about 500mm (20in) square which would go into a linen bag. This is a real scrollsaw job, and although I have shown symmetrical cuts you can do them to a free pattern. Children love giant jigsaw puzzles, and they will get added enjoyment from making up the board before starting to play with the farm.

Because the buildings sit on the base board make their floors out of 3mm MDF

Britannia farm animals

The Big Barn completed

or hardboard and you may, if you wish, extend the floors forward as a paved area.

A much lighter-weight alternative would be to use a piece of deck canvas, or similar material, that can be rolled up and put away. The material should be sized with a watered-down solution of PVA or other glue and then flatted with a white emulsion matt paint. On this you can then paint the layout in coloured acrylic paints.

Medium Sized Board

A more practical solution, especially for the smaller home, is to make the farm yard board 1000mm x 750mm x 9mm (39in x 29$\frac{1}{2}$in x $\frac{3}{8}$in) and place the buildings on the floor around it. The bases for the different buildings are made from 9mm ($\frac{3}{8}$in) MDF, so that their ground floors are level with the farmyard. This is the system illustrated here.

Layout

Paint the board with flat white emulsion paint. Divide it into 100mm (4in) squares and draw the layout in pencil. Paint the outside squares a grey concrete colour and paving slabs may be drawn on them. There is a ring road for lorries and other vehicles to circulate. The roads are 100mm wide with a grassy central plot and duck pond. As the farm develops the house may go at the top right hand corner, hence the footpath to the front door, and perhaps later on a grain hopper will stand on the grass by the gate – but the layout is up to you.

You are now ready to start making your farm buildings and the method of construction is the same throughout.

1 Make the walls from 6mm ($\frac{1}{4}$in) plywood or MDF. The end walls contain the floor and the long walls sit upon it. This sets the building up square and true. Cut the floor for each building to the outside width but to a length that is 12mm less than the outside length. The end walls are made 9mm higher than the long (front & back) walls so that they drop down over the floor.

2 To form the corner joints glue and pin small battens to the end walls and set them in by the thickness of the long walls (6mm in this case). If you have a rip saw it is easy to cut 9mm ($\frac{3}{8}$in) square battens from waste pieces, or you can buy 9mm quadrant moulding, or pine strip from a hardware store. If you are making a two-storey building, space is left for the floor to slot between the vertical battens. Fix horizontal battens to carry the upper floor. Note how the floorboard is notched to accept the end wall battens. These small notches are very easy to cut with the scrollsaw.

3 The roof may be fixed or removable. If the roof lifts off, the children can put animals in their stalls and it affords storage space for the model animals when the farm is stowed away. A removable roof such as the one on the big barn is illustrated below. The roof trusses are cut to the exact shape of the end walls as solid triangles of MDF/plywood and glued and pinned to the roof panels. For a large roof a ridge piece gives added strength and this may be ornamental. Battens or trusses at each end locate the roof so that it drops on like a box lid.

View looking down on Big Barn with roof removed

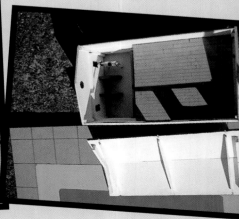

Looking into the Big Barn with ro[of] and first floor panel removed

4 Roof pitches vary a lot. Corrugated iron, aluminium and asbestos roofs are quite flat (14° pitch), whereas tiled roofs are much steeper (28° pitch). The dimensions given on the drawings establish the eaves and ridge heights for each building to give suitable slopes. Flat roofs need not be removable.

The Big Barn

This important building contains a stable, garage and central unloading bay so that the child can start to play right away. It also introduces all the different aspects of construction. It has a removable roof and a lift-up panel in the first floor to access the stable. It may have the stable at either end (see Patterns).

5 Cut the 9mm baseboard 438mm long x 250mm wide (17in x 9in). From 6mm (¼in) plywood cut the two long walls 438mm x 189mm (17in x 7⅜in) and the two end walls 250mm (17in) x 189mm (7⅜in) high to eaves and 225mm (8⅞in) high at mid-point.

6 Mark out the door and window positions from the drawing and cut them out on the scrollsaw. Drill holes so that they accept the saw blade for the window cutouts and take particular care to make the corners square.

7 Glue and pin 9mm (⅜in) square vertical battens (or quadrant moulding) to the end walls. Set them in by the thickness of the front and back walls and leave gaps for the first floor panel to drop in.

8 Glue and pin horizontal battens to the walls to carry the first floor.

NOTE for model makers:
If you intend to buy prefabricated ¹/₂₄th windows and doors, make sure that the openings conform exactly to the manufacturer's sizes.

General views of the first stage with the big barn, animals & machinery on medium-sized board

9 Offer the end wall panels up to the floor and mark out the notches in the floor for the vertical battens. Cut them out with the scroll saw.

10 Cut the ground floor partitions 236mm x 114mm (9in x 4in) from hardboard or 3mm MDF and fix battens on the long walls to locate them.

11 Cut the panel for the first floor 438mm x 237mm (17in x 9⅜in) from hardboard/MDF. If you want to have access to the stable from above make that end of the floor removable. After painting to a natural wood colour draw lines for the floorboards. Two pieces of 9mm MDF 70mm x 50mm (2⅞in x 2in) may be fixed to the floor in the stable to form stalls for the horses.
TIP: It is a good idea at this stage before final assembly to give all surfaces a flat white undercoat.

12 Glue the building together using a cord or frame clamp (tourniquet) round the four walls.

13 Glue in the partitions, stable dividers and the fixed part of the first floor.

14 Cut four roof trusses from 9mm (⅜in) MDF/plywood. Copy exactly the triangular shape of the end wall gables and notch them at the apex to accept the ridge piece. They must just fit inside the walls. For appearance, the roof should be longer than the barn and should overhang at the eaves. Cut two roof panels 464mm (18in) x 140mm (5in) x 6mm (¼in). Chamfer at the apex with a sanding block or plane to fit tightly against the ridge piece.

15 Cut the ridge piece 464mm (18¼in) long. If you wish to make the attractive ornamental ridge with end finials this will come out of a width of 50mm (2in). It has to be set out very accurately to the dimensions given on the drawing and 10mm (⁷/₁₆in) holes drilled at 18mm (¹¹/₁₆in) centres. The scalloped top is cut out on the saw. A plain ridge piece would come out of a 35mm (1³/₈in) wide strip.

16 Glue up the roof. Make sure it fits firmly on to the walls and lifts off easily. Finish painting and varnishing all round.

Materials and Finishes

There is no doubt that birch-faced ply is the most attractive material for the scroll saw user, but it costs more and if you are going to paint over the surfaces later then a cheaper plywood, hardboard or MDF will suffice. MDF is smooth on both faces with a fine uniform texture throughout, but edges may break if nails or screws are placed too near them without prior drilling. It swells when moist and is highly absorbent, drinking up sealers or other finishes greedily. Many timber yards supply 4ft square sheets that can be brought home in the car. Hardboard is low-priced and is useful for roofs, partitions and smaller buildings.

On small work like this it is good craftsmanship to drill pilot holes (1.5mm) for panel pins in one of the pieces to be joined. This prevents splitting and makes assembly and easy.

I have found Perma-grit abrasive materials extremely long lasting and easy to use. Because they are mounted on metal they come half way between fine files and sandpaper.

Mix student quality acrylic paints with white emulsion, or use colour dyes to obtain the different colours. Black, red, blue and yellow will make any colour you need and this is an inexpensive way of decorating items such as this. After completion give the whole project a few coats of clear varnish such as Rustin's Plastic Coating, or acrylic varnish. For realism, you may prefer to paint the roads with a thin adhesive and sprinkle silver sand on them.

If you wish to make windows yourself try thin acetate sheet with painted white bars or white tape. For model villages and railway layouts opening doors are not

essential but for a farmyard the child will want to put horses into stables and vehicles into sheds or the garage.

Surface textures and finishes also offer you a choice of three systems. The accurate model maker may purchase printed papers, or better still embossed plastic sheets to portray roof tiles, brickwork, random stone walling etc. You can make textured surfaces yourself. There are modeling clays that can be worked to form artificial stone. Another method is to coat the surface with a thin (2mm or less) coating of cellulose filler and when it reaches the right consistency scribe with a cocktail stick tiles, blocks or random stonework patterns into the paste for painting afterwards with matt colours. Finally the simplest system of all, the one illustrated here, for a child's plaything is simply to leave the openings and paint the models in bold simple colours. Realism costs much more, but it depends upon your objective.

Whichever line you adopt you can rest assured that you would be creating a lively and interesting model. The children will enjoy setting it up and arranging their buildings in different ways and at the end of the day you can pop the animals inside the big barn roof and put it away quickly.

SUPPLIERS LIST
Tools, Materials and Colour Dyes
- **Axminster Power Tools, Chard Street, Axminster, Devon EX13 5DZ Tel: 0800 371822**
- **Boddy's, Boroughbridge, North Yorkshire YO5 9LJ Tel: 01423-322370**
- **Craft Supplies Ltd., Miller's Dale, Buxton, Derbyshire SK17 8SN Tel: 01298-871636**

Abrasives
- **Perma-Grit Tools, The White House, Pointon, Sleaford, Lincs. NG34 0LX Tel: 0800-2985121**
- **General Scrollsaw Supplies**
- **Hobby's (Dereham) Ltd., Dereham, Norfolk NR19 2QZ Tel: 01362-692985**
- **W. Hobby Ltd., Knight's Hill Square, London SE27 0HH Tel: 0208-7614244**

Doll's House Specialists
- **Jackson's Miniatures, 6 Anderson Close, Epsom, Surrey KT19 8LY Tel: 01372-739363**

CUTTING LIST

Item	No	Length mm	Length in	Width mm	Width in	Thickness mm	Thickness in	Material
Ground floor base	1	438	17$^{1}/_{4}$	250	9$^{3}/_{4}$	9	$^{3}/_{8}$	MDF/Plywood
Front and back walls	2	438	17$^{1}/_{4}$	189	7$^{3}/_{8}$	6	$^{1}/_{4}$	MDF/plywood
End walls	2	250	9$^{3}/_{4}$	225	8$^{7}/_{8}$	6	$^{1}/_{4}$	MDF/Plywood
Upper floor	1	438	17$^{1}/_{4}$	238	9$^{3}/_{8}$	3	$^{1}/_{8}$	Hardboard/MDF
Partitions	2	236	9$^{1}/_{4}$	114	4$^{1}/_{2}$	3	$^{1}/_{8}$	Hardboard/MDF
Stalls	2	70	2$^{3}/_{4}$	50	2	9	$^{3}/_{8}$	MDF
Roof Panels	2	464	18$^{1}/_{4}$	140	5$^{1}/_{2}$	6	$^{1}/_{4}$	MDF/plywood
Roof Trusses	4	250	9$^{3}/_{4}$	150	6	9	$^{3}/_{8}$	MDF
Ridge	1	464	18$^{1}/_{4}$	50	2	3	$^{1}/_{8}$	MDF/hardboard

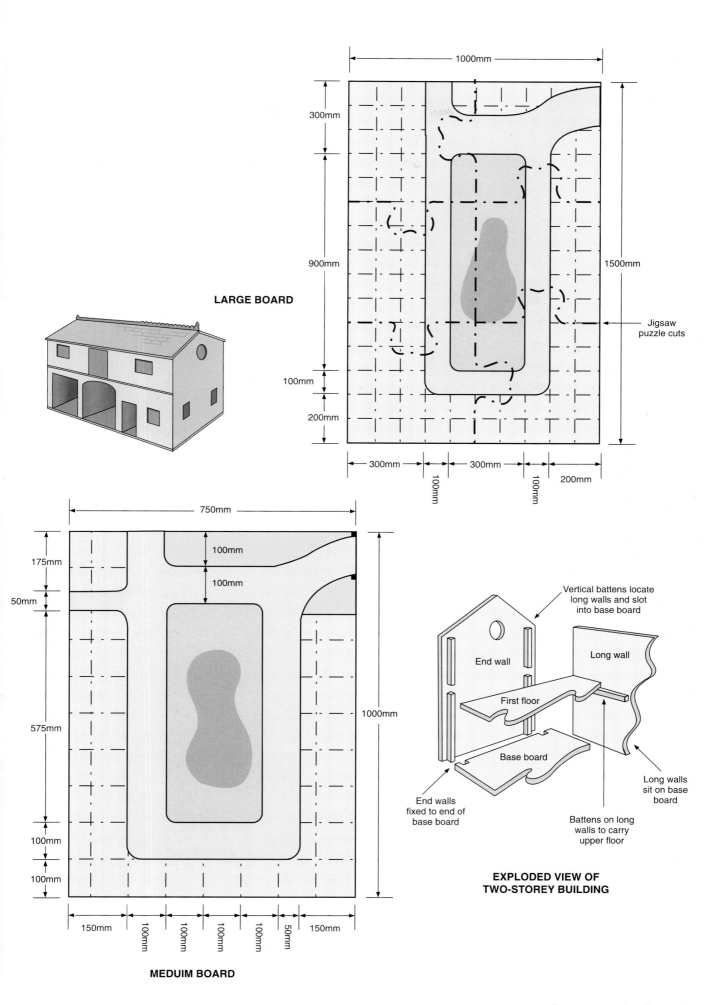

LARGE BOARD

1000mm

300mm

900mm

100mm

200mm

1500mm

Jigsaw puzzle cuts

300mm

300mm

100mm

100mm

200mm

MEDUIM BOARD

750mm

175mm

50mm

575mm

100mm

100mm

100mm

100mm

1000mm

150mm

100mm

100mm

100mm

100mm

50mm

150mm

Vertical battens locate long walls and slot into base board

End wall

Long wall

First floor

Base board

Long walls sit on base board

End walls fixed to end of base board

Battens on long walls to carry upper floor

EXPLODED VIEW OF TWO-STOREY BUILDING

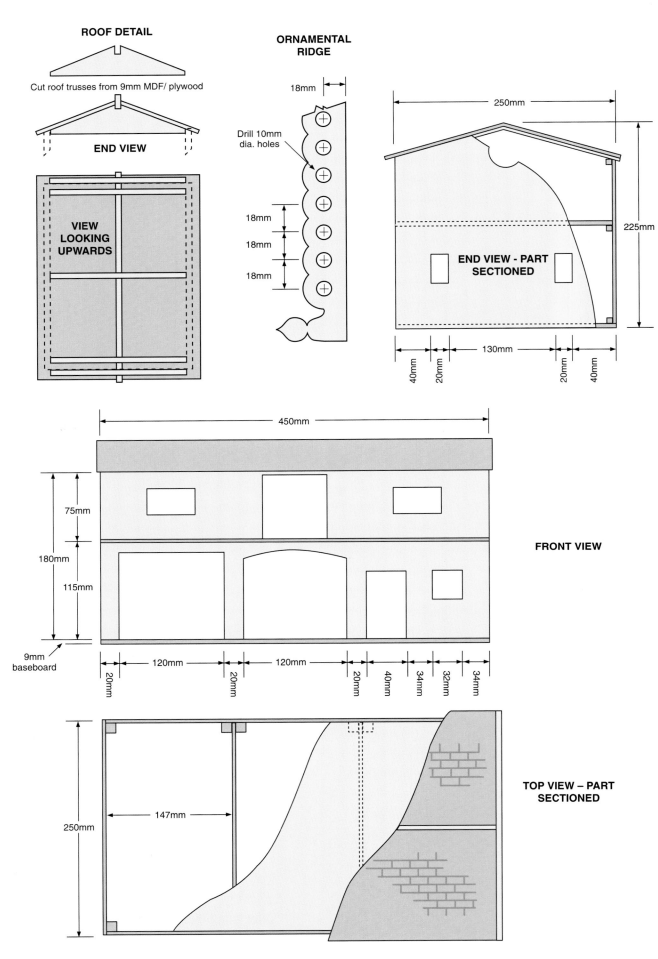

ROOF DETAIL

Cut roof trusses from 9mm MDF/ plywood

END VIEW

VIEW LOOKING UPWARDS

ORNAMENTAL RIDGE

18mm

Drill 10mm dia. holes

18mm
18mm
18mm

250mm

END VIEW - PART SECTIONED

225mm

40mm 20mm 130mm 20mm 40mm

450mm

75mm

180mm

115mm

FRONT VIEW

9mm baseboard

20mm 120mm 20mm 120mm 20mm 40mm 34mm 32mm 34mm

250mm

147mm

TOP VIEW – PART SECTIONED

All aboard the orient

John Everett
shows how to
make a Japanese-
style shelf unit

This project came about as a result of needing somewhere to display a collection of assorted knick-knacks – you know the sort of thing – we've all got them laying around gathering dust, wanting somewhere to sit and look attractive. This design is based loosely on the open frame multiple box type of thing that was popular in the 1960s. It was made originally from slats of wood with slots cut half way into each slat and the whole

thing was simply slotted together to make up a framework with the ends sticking out fashionably.

In order to make the design somewhat original, it was redesigned in a sort of Japanese style with regular geometric patterns incised into all the upright sections of the shelf unit and a back panel for wall fixing was added, again with incised designs in order to finish the thing off in a more modern style. The incised designs are all cut out on the scrollsaw as are the panels that go to make up the complete shelf unit. The finished unit was decorated in dark maroon with gold trim to mimic the rich finish of similar oriental pieces which are lacquered in this fashion. You can, of course, use whatever decoration you prefer but this is the one used here.

> "The incised
> designs are all
> cut out on the
> scrollsaw as
> are the panels
> that go to
> make up the
> complete shelf
> unit"

mark out the positions for the starter holes for your blade. It is easier to make these starter holes adjacent to an internal right angle in the design so that the start and finish of each cut will always match up precisely.

1 ▲ **By laying out the cutting patterns on the sheet material – in this case 6mm MDF – it is easy to save material by interlocking the individual parts of the shelf unit before cutting out the blanks.**

2 **Use small pieces of double-sided tape to stick the blanks together where two identical parts are required such as the main shelves, the centre and end uprights. The two parts needed can now be cut out at the same time which not only saves time, it means that both parts will be identical even if there are any minor deviations from the** ◀ **cutting pattern.**

3 **With the parts which have the incised design, such as the back panel and the uprights of the shelf unit, you will need to** ▼

Materials, tools

To make up the shelf unit, you will need the following materials and tools:

- 6mm MDF or ply, whichever you prefer or have available. The dimensions for the individual parts as follows:
  Top shelf – 143mm x 100mm (5¾in x 4in) – cut one
  Main shelves – 355mm x 100mm (14in x 4in) – cut two
  Centre uprights – 290mm x 100mm (11⅜in x 4in) – cut two
  End uprights – 168mm x 100mm (6⅝in x 4in) – cut two
  Back panel – 325mm x 262mm (12¾in x 10⁵⁄₁₆in) – cut one
- Spraymount adhesive or rubber cement, etc.
- Wood glue
- Brass panel pins
- Mirror screws for fixing in position for wall-mounted version
- Decorating materials of your choice. The example shown here was painted with a primer/sealer coat of white acrylic and then finished with deep maroon enamel and gold trim
- Skip-tooth scrollsaw blade of about size 5 to make negotiating the right-angled turns a simple affair. A coarser blade will produce a more rounded corner which will necessitate cleaning up after sawing with a file

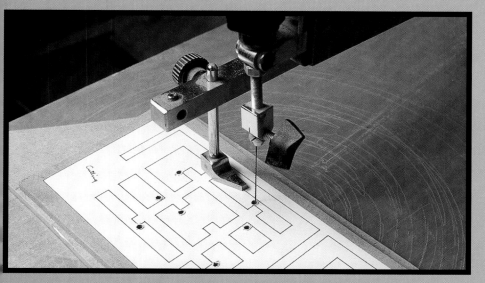

4 ▲ The scrollsaw is set up to make the series of internal cutouts on the main uprights of the shelf unit. Note that the hold-down device has been set to prevent workpiece 'chatter' which would otherwise occur when turning around all the right angles in the design.

5 The internal design ▶ taking shape as more and more of the internal cutouts are completed. At this point the oriental-style design begins to become apparent.

6 With the internal cutouts completed on the 'stack' being cut, the external cut is made. ▼ Take care when cutting the

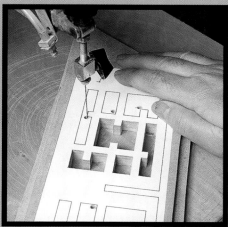

slots that will allow the uprights to join the actual shelves. Do not be tempted to make them larger than they should be for an easier fit or it will be difficult to maintain everything in perfect square once the assembly stage is reached. It is much better to follow your cutting line accurately and then,

if necessary, remove small amounts of material with a flat file after cutting is complete to ensure a perfect fit. Don't try to be in too much of a hurry to complete the project or you will inevitably run into problems.

7 With the cutting completed, remove the remains of the cutting patterns and clean up any remains of the adhesive left over from sticking the pattern in place. Any residue of adhesive will quickly clog up sandpaper and will be a nuisance at this point. ▼

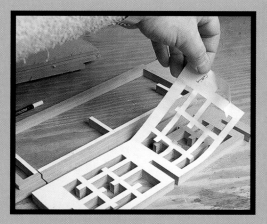

8 Using a scrap piece of MDF removed during the cutting out as a quick check on the fitting accuracy of each half of the slots. It is best to use a scrap piece of the same material for this purpose as it will avoid damage if the two halves of a ▼

slotted joint which are a little tight in fit are pushed together with a bit too much force. All the slots can be checked in this way prior to assembling the completed shelf unit.

holes for the mirror screws which will be used to fix the completed shelf unit to a wall. Check that the size drill bit you use actually suits the size of mirror screw you have to hand.

are within the limits of even a modestly sized scrollsaw. You have to bear in mind the longest possible dimension to be found on the back panel which will be a diagonal line and if the amount of external waste to be cut away is any more than an absolute minimum, then you could well run into problems when trying to negotiate the work piece around the blade to make the internal cutouts. ▼

9 When you come to make the internal cutouts on the back panel of the unit, you will also need ▼ to drill and countersink two

10 With the back panel, the external cutouts are made first so that the overall dimensions of the work piece

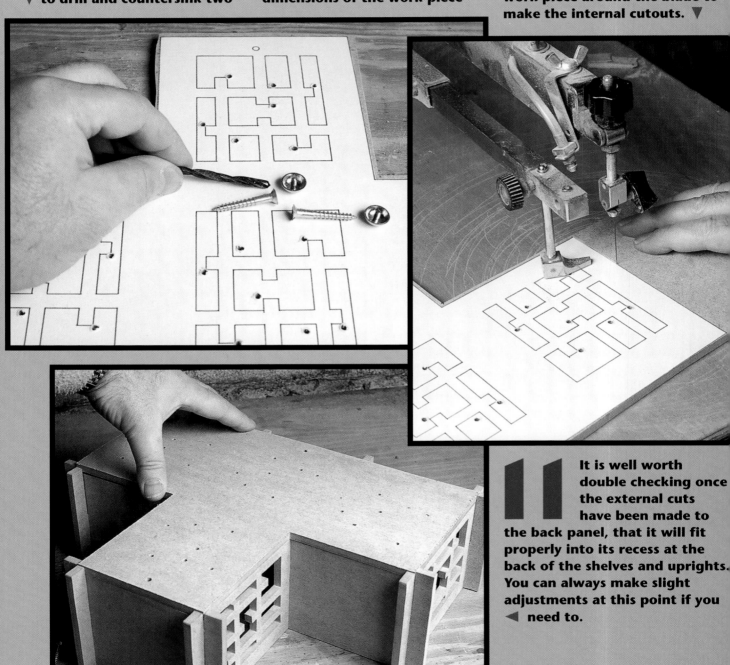

11 It is well worth double checking once the external cuts have been made to the back panel, that it will fit properly into its recess at the back of the shelves and uprights. You can always make slight adjustments at this point if you ◄ need to.

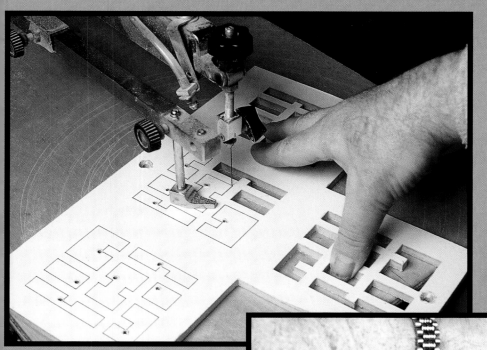

glue and tack everything together with brass panel pins. It is worth the effort to make pilot holes for the panel pins to avoid any splitting that might otherwise occur. A mini-drill is excellent for this purpose if you have one.

14 Making the pilot holes for the panel pins with a tiny drill bit fitted to a mini-drill. ▼

12 ▲ The internal cutouts well under way on the back panel of the unit. This panel has the most internal cutouts to do and will require a little patience but the results will be worth the effort.

13 ◄ With everything cut out and having been checked for fit in a dry run, you can now begin assembling the shelf unit. Use a light smear of wood

15 The fully decorated unit in position on the wall and laden with a selection of ◄ favourite ornaments.

142mm

355mm

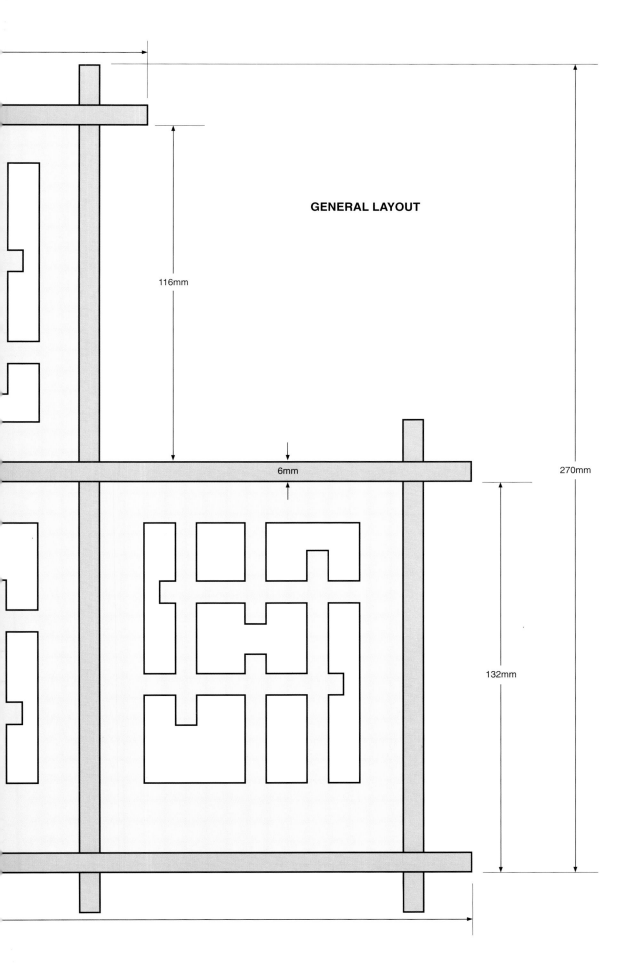

GENERAL LAYOUT

116mm

6mm

270mm

132mm

BACK PANEL

A – Clearance hole +
countersink for mirror
screws to fix to wall

112.5mm

325mm

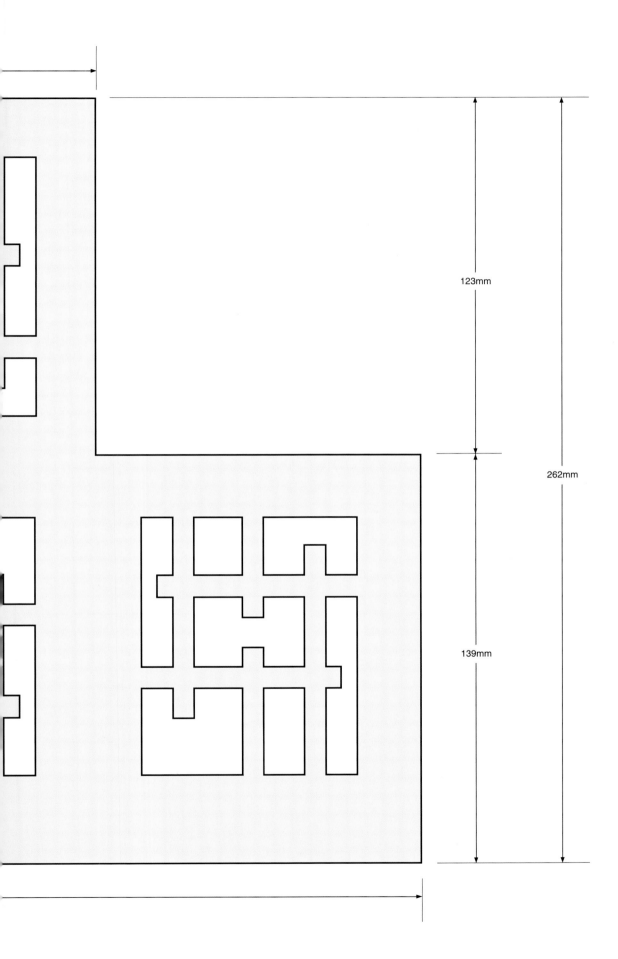

123mm

262mm

139mm

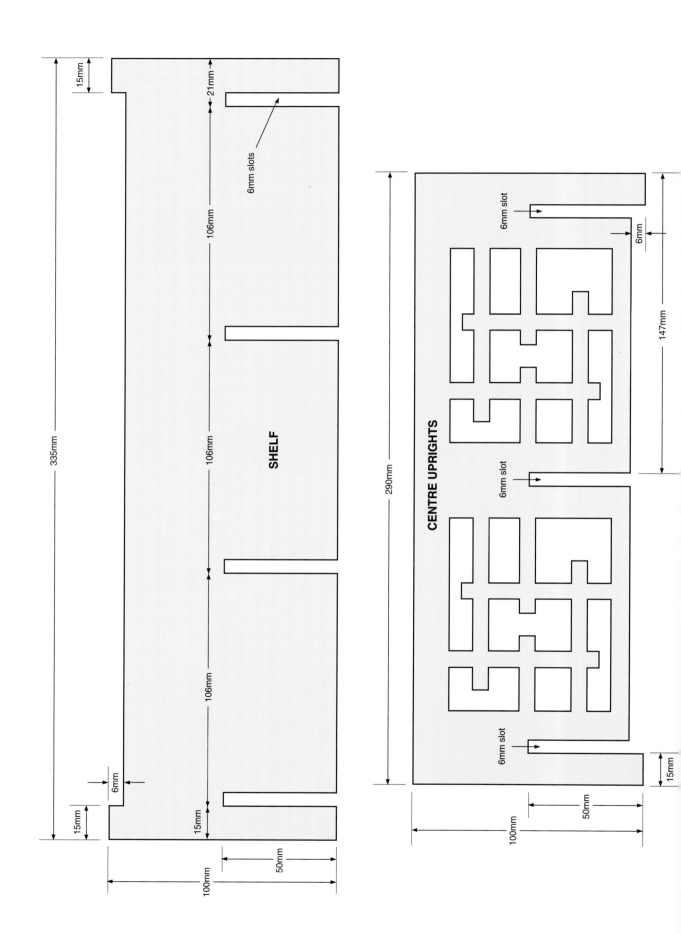

SHELF

CENTRE UPRIGHTS

6mm slots

15mm
21mm
106mm
106mm
106mm
335mm
6mm
15mm
15mm
100mm
50mm

6mm slot
6mm
147mm
290mm
6mm slot
6mm slot
15mm
100mm
50mm

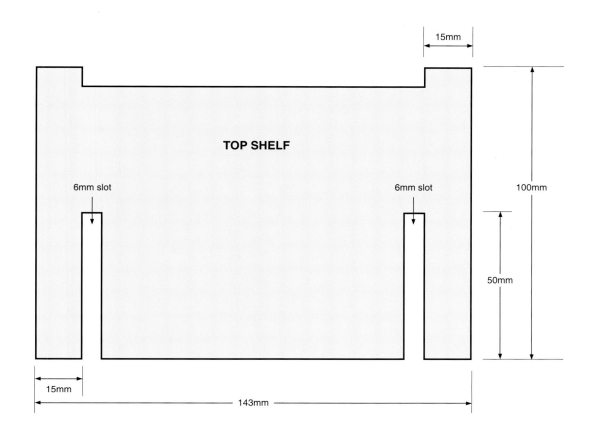

TOP SHELF

6mm slot

6mm slot

15mm

100mm

50mm

15mm

143mm

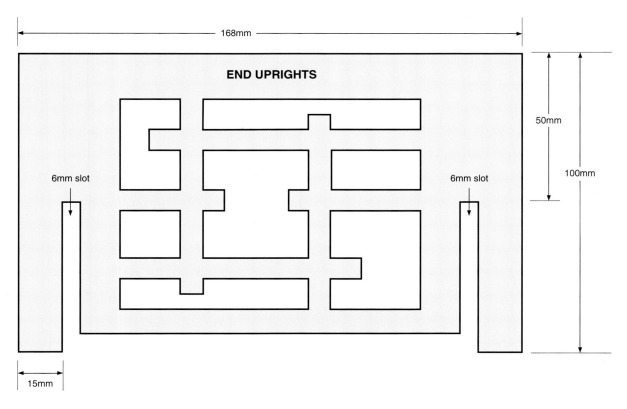

168mm

END UPRIGHTS

6mm slot

6mm slot

50mm

100mm

15mm

Display shelves for a special toy make tidying up less of a chore says **Christine Richardson**

Obeying battle orders

Materials and tools

Cutting list
- 6mm birch plywood
  1 @ 50 x 340mm
  1 @ 150 x 340mm
- 18mm prepared pine
  2 @ 145 x 310mm
  2 @ 145 x 450mm
- Pine quadrant moulding
  4 @ 145mm

Because this project requires exact measurements, we have not converted to imperial.

Materials
- Panel pins
- Natural stone-fleck spray paint
- Wood glue
- Red and yellow enamel or acrylic paint
- Spraymount adhesive

Tools
- Scrollsaw blades:
  20 tpi for timber 2 to 13mm ($5/64$ to $1/2$in) thick
  Speedline 5 tpi with return teeth, for timber 30mm ($1 3/16$in) or more thick
- Hammer
- Handsaw
- Drill with small bit
- Square
- Small clamp

Some toys, like these great Lego® characters, are just not meant to be put away, but to encourage tidy behaviour in young warriors it's a good idea to provide a special place to display their building skills.

Requiring only a simple construction technique and basic tools, this small and wall-mountable castle-style shelf is easy to build with a basic tool kit.

1 Ask the timber yard to cut the wood to size (*see cutting list*). The measurements are exact because the edges must be square and will require no further processing of the timber. If the yard cannot guarantee this, then ask for an additional 6mm on each length, and make final adjustments with a square and handsaw. The quadrant

moulding is normally sold in full lengths which must be cut to size.

2 Mark out the castellations for the top of the castle wall on one end of each of the two long pieces of pine. Castellations of 29mm square will fit exactly. Clearly mark the waste area to be cut out.

Using the 5 tpi blade, make all the vertical cuts for the sides and then, with the scrollsaw turned off, slide the blade down to the bottom of one cut. Turn on the scrollsaw and, keeping the blade in the same position, slowly rotate the work to leave a small amount of waste in the corner.

Cut all the way across the bottom of the waste area to meet the bottom of the next vertical cut. Most of the waste is now free and can be moved out of the way, but you may need to turn off the scrollsaw again to do this. Turn the work around and cut towards the small amount of waste left in the first corner. The waste should come away cleanly. Repeat for each castellation.

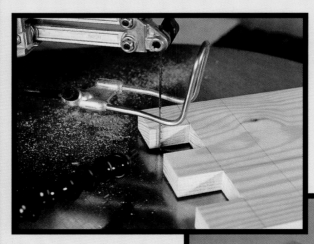

Cut out castellations in the side pieces, making all the vertical cuts first

◄ Saw out castellations and windows

◄ Blade threaded ready to saw out a cross-shaped window

3 Make a photocopy of the design template (*see end of article*), and enlarge by the stated percentage. Spray the larger piece of plywood with adhesive and attach the photocopy. Using a small drill bit, drill holes in the corner of each arched window and drill a hole at all four corners of the cross-shaped windows. Release the tension and remove the blade from the top blade clamp. Thread the 20 tpi blade through one of these holes, clamp the blade and tension it. Remove the waste. Repeat for each window.

Repeat the process for the ▶ **second tower and leave the centre turret and flag until last**

4 First, remove the waste between the castellations on both towers, and then carefully remove waste between the turret and larger

tower. The area of the flag pole is weak and should be treated with care when cutting out.

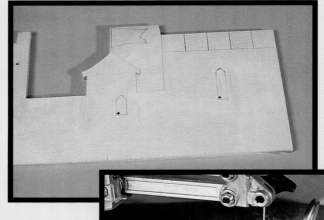

Make all the vertical cuts for the castellations before attempting to remove any waste in between them ▼

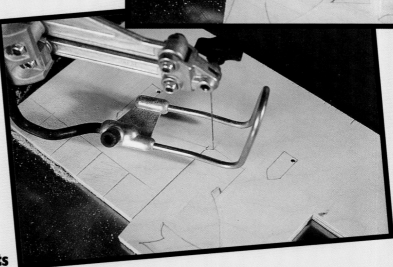

"The area of the flag pole is weak and should be treated with care when cutting out"

◄ Cutting out the turret area; note the small amount of waste in the corner behind the blade, to be cut out later

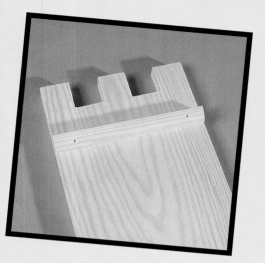

Pin quadrant moulding onto side pieces ▶

"The measurements are exact because the edges must be square and will require no further processing of the timber"

5 Using a square, mark the position of the shelves at 60mm and 400mm from the top on each side piece. With the castellations on the left, and using a piece of waste timber, clamp up the work face on a table or bench. The waste timber should lie along the line drawn for the shelf position, and acts as a stop for the quadrant while it is being pinned to the side piece, ensuring that the shelves are at right angles.

Glue along one flat side of quadrant and attach with panel pins. Repeat until all four pieces of the quadrant are attached, ready to support the shelves.

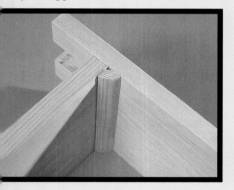

▲ Showing the position of the quadrant moulding under shelf and on side piece

6 With castellations to the left, lay one side piece face up on the bench. Take one shelf, decide which is the top surface, and on one end glue both edges where it will rest on the quadrant and meet the side piece. Position the shelf and pin through the quadrant into the bottom of the shelf. Repeat for the second shelf.

7 Clamp the second shelf support on the bench as with the first. Being careful not to strain the newly glued and pinned joints, pick up the other side with the two

shelves attached and place them in position on the second side piece. Fix the edges of the shelves to the side as before, gluing and pinning from underneath.

8 Before these joints are set, attach the bottom rail behind the bottom shelf, level with its top edge. Then attach the rail sides to the side pieces. Attach the top rail, with the scrollsawn design uppermost, placing its bottom edge level with the bottom of the top shelf. The sides are now braced and held square by the top and bottom rail. Leave the glue to dry.

9 Apply woodfiller to any gaps where the shelves meet the sides or quadrant, sand when dry and remove any nibs of wood. The example shown here is finished with a spray-on paint that simulates stone. No priming or undercoating is necessary.

10 To spray paint, first mask off the flag and flag pole. Take your work outside, and protect anything near the spraying area with cardboard. Spray

the undersides of the shelves and then stand the piece upright and work around it. Do not spray the back of the shelves or the rails. Spray in short, even, downward strokes that are slightly overlapping. Do not apply too much paint at once as this retards the drying process. Leave to dry.

11 Remove the masking tape and draw a simple design on the flag. Using a small brush, apply acrylic or enamel paint and leave to dry.

If you want to hang the shelves on the wall, wait until the work is dry and finish off by spraying the bottom of the sides.

Hanging shelves

To hang the shelves, either drill two holes in the top rail close to the shelf and hang on round-headed screws, or attach a mirror plate to each side about one-third of the way down.

The unit after assembly. Any gaps between the quadrant and shelves ▼ are filled before painting

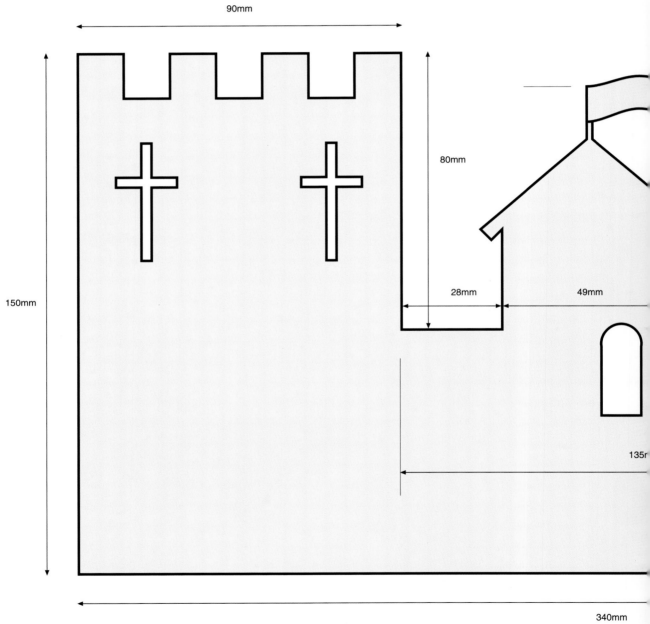

90mm

80mm

150mm

28mm

49mm

135r

340mm

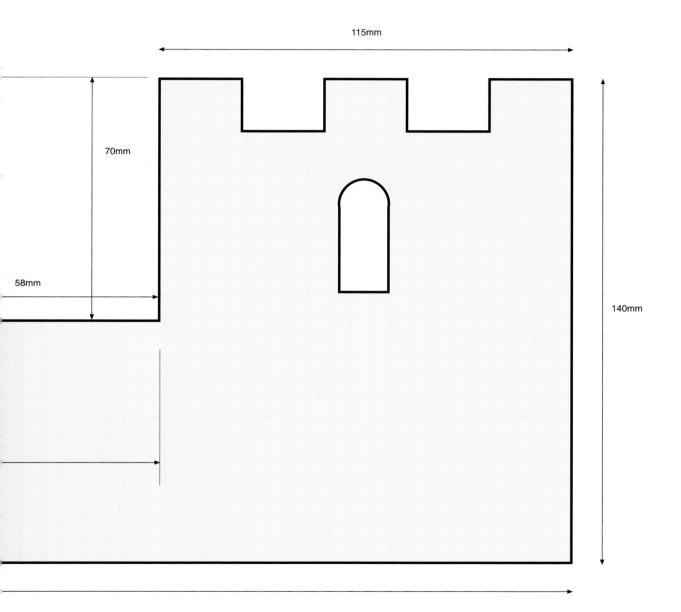

115mm

70mm

58mm

140mm

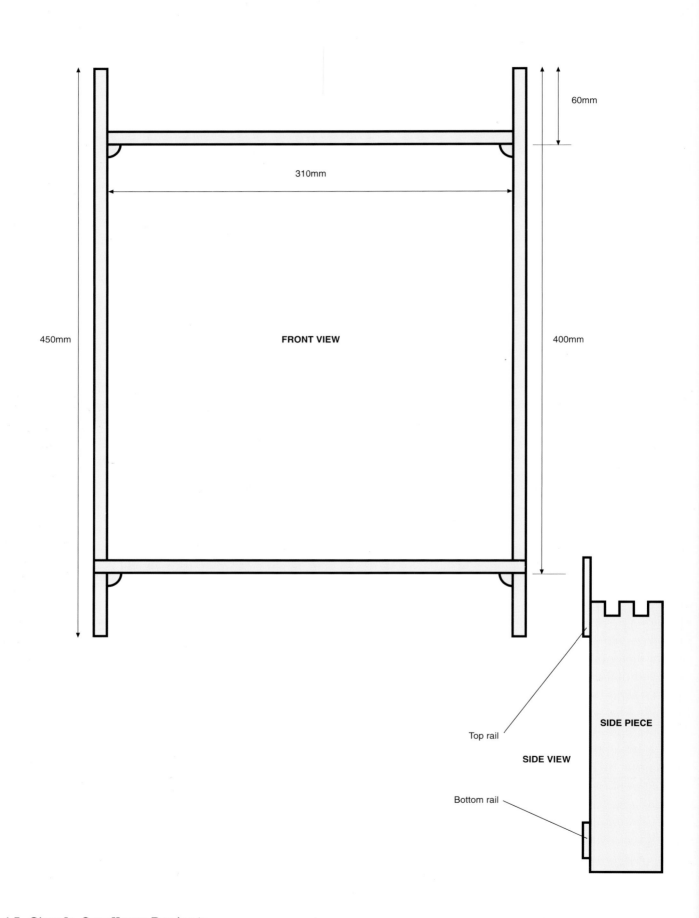

450mm

60mm

310mm

FRONT VIEW

400mm

Top rail

SIDE VIEW

SIDE PIECE

Bottom rail

Glorious windows

Based on posters from Alphonse Mucha, **Terry Lawrence** creates some stylish acrylic window hangings

I love to experiment with transparent Altuglas cast acrylic sheets, and have often used it to make multi-layered jigsaws – and it is much easier to use than you might think.

Seven colours are available in the transparent range – 3mm (⅛in) thick – and I set out to create a decoration for a plain window, where daylight will shine through the colours.

In this project there are two interpretations of posters designed by Alphonse Mucha in the 1890s. One is a portrait of the actress Sarah Bernhardt and the other is taken from an 1894 design for a calendar commissioned by the magazine 'La Plume', which was then published in Paris.

For each, I have simplified the detail considerably and have used only two

colours. It is therefore possible to cut each from just two pieces of acrylic sheet.

Both designs are 270mm (10⅝in) diameter, so they can be made on the smallest scroll saw. I found that a relatively coarse blade (No 5) was best, used at 300–600 rpm though, if you have only a fixed speed saw, the blade dimensions and number of teeth per inch, are more important than the speed.

Finer blades, I find, tend to produce a cut edge which needs either scraping or polishing.

Portrait of Sarah Bernhardt

Mucha's first portrait of Sarah was in 1895, but the one I have chosen is an interpretation of 'Tête Byzantine', painted when Sarah had just turned 50. I have changed her neckline (taking off about 10 years) but even without this cosmetic touch, she beats, I think, most of the modern lot!

For this piece, I used amber acrylic for the circular base and red for the overlay.

1 Enlarge the patterns by photocopier to full size (270mm diameter) or to whatever size you prefer.

Altuglas has a protective film on both sides; one white and one blue. The white may be drawn upon with ballpoint pen, at least sufficiently well for the first concentric circles of the base rim.

2 To describe the outline, first fix a scrap of 4mm (⁵⁄₃₂in) MDF or wood to the acrylic (with its white side up). Place the scrap at the approximate centre of the circle to be drawn and hold it with masking tape. You may then use compasses to draw the inner and outer circles (10mm (⅜in) apart) without the point marking the acrylic.

3 Cut out the 270mm (10⅝in) disc and, with carbon paper below your drawing, you can trace the outline of the head. The carboned lines should be sufficiently defined to follow with your saw blade but, if not, you can draw over them with a ballpoint pen. Red and the

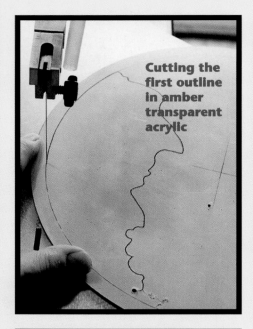

Cutting the first outline in amber transparent acrylic

Base piece, and shoulder piece, both cut from the same colour

▲ Second layer (ruby red) being pierced with headband design

other darker colours are not so easy and I will describe later a better method for these.

4 Cut around the outline shown; there are only three areas to be removed. Leave the shoulder outline intact as the lines at 8 o'clock are those of an extra piece of amber acrylic, to represent the folds of Sarah's dress.

5 The eye is a single cut (I used a No 2 blade here, but it's not critical) using a fine drill bit (0.5mm) at the corner of the eye to thread the blade through. This fine drill was mounted in a pin chuck, which then fitted into the chuck of my pillar drill. All drilling

should be done with a sharp bit, at low rpm and with light pressure, to avoid a raised lower rim to the hole.

6 The hairpiece with byzantine piercing was cut from a single piece of red acrylic, 270mm x 190mm (10⅝in x 7⅝in) minimum size. As you see, my cartoon has modified the shapes of the decorative headband and the ear-rings, to allow a one-piece overlay. Even so, it is a nice exercise in careful fretwork.

To ensure a clear cutting line, cover the acrylic (still with its protective plastic films) with self-adhesive paper address labels. Tracing the lines onto this white surface with carbon paper yielded a good line. Drawing direct onto the white film can give a line which can be rubbed off with the touch of a finger, so play safe!

Red overlay completed, with matching lips ▼

▼ Close-up of Sarah

7 First, cut the outline of the piece. The lips can be cut later from scrap. My drawings of amber base and red overlay match in outline, so if you have changed a line in your amber base, then adjust your drawing on the red to match.

8 Now drill for all cutouts. I used a 1mm (¹⁄₁₆in) drill bit for these, again mounted in a pin chuck. A No 5 blade can be used throughout, yielding a clean, almost polished edge. Any edge whitening can be smoothed with a scalpel blade (Swann-Morton No 3 handle with No 10A blade, are ideal).

9 Cut the shoulder overlay from amber acrylic, checking the line at the point where it meets the vertical red hairline, to ensure matching curves which will butt together.

All that remains is to peel the protective films from the cut pieces and assemble with adhesive. For laminating, Tensol 70 is specified and I also ordered a special applicator for this. I found that the 'applicator' kit, from Evode who make the Tensol, was grossly overpriced and completely useless for laminating transparents. If you wish, experiment with the product yourself to see how it works for you.

I experimented with several methods and with both Tensol 12 and 70. Even with pressure, you cannot avoid visible glue marks, rather like little transparent jellyfish. I found that the best method was to spot-weld with dots of mixed (two-part) Tensol 70 at several points on the rim of the circle and also one at the spot where the hairline meets the neck.

Press together and leave for an hour, after adding the shoulder overlay and the lips.

10 You can drill the rim at a point where the piece will hang correctly and suspend with nylon monofilament fishing line.

▲ First cut of La Demoiselle de la Plume (plastic protective film attached)

For the green and amber
Demoiselle de la Plume

The procedures are exactly the same, as my sequence of photos show. I intended to use transparent yellow for the base, but it proved very insipid and the green was too strong a contrast with it. However, the rich viridian green is modified by the amber to a much warmer shade, close to Hooker's green light, in watercolour terms.

Original cartoon overlaid on green acrylic. Carbon paper is used to transfer design to aper covering ▼

▲ Green overlay design transferred, ready for drilling of waste sections

▲ Overlay cutting completed (protective film attached)

▲ Overlay stripped ready for laminating

BASE (AMBER)

OVERLAY (RED)

BASE (AMBER)

OVERLAY (GREEN)

Metric/Imperial Conversion Chart

mm	inch	mm	inch	mm	inch	mm	inch
1	0.03937	27	1.06299	80	3.14960	340	13.38582
2	0.07874	28	1.10236	90	3.54330	350	13.77952
3	0.11811	29	1.14173	100	3.93700		
4	0.15748	30	1.18110			360	14.17322
5	0.19685			110	4.33070	370	14.56692
		31	1.22047	120	4.72440	380	14.96063
6	0.23622	32	1.25984	130	5.11811	390	15.35433
7	0.27559	33	1.29921	140	5.51181	400	15.74803
8	0.31496	34	1.33858	150	5.90551		
9	0.35433	35	1.37795			410	16.14173
10	0.39370			160	6.29921	420	16.53543
		36	1.41732	170	6.69291	430	16.92913
11	0.43307	37	1.45669	180	7.08661	440	17.32283
12	0.47244	38	1.49606	190	7.48031	450	17.71653
13	0.51181	39	1.53543	200	7.87401		
14	0.55118	40	1.57480			460	18.11023
15	0.59055			210	8.26771	470	18.50393
		41	1.61417	220	8.66141	480	18.89763
16	0.62992	42	1.65354	230	9.05511	490	19.29133
17	0.66929	43	1.69291	240	9.44881	500	19.68504
18	0.70866	44	1.73228	250	9.84252		
19	0.74803	45	1.77165				
20	0.78740			260	10.23622		
		46	1.81102	270	10.62992		
21	0.82677	47	1.85039	280	11.02362		
22	0.86614	48	1.88976	290	11.41732		
23	0.90551	49	1.92913	300	11.81102		
24	0.94488	50	1.96850	310	12.20472		
25	0.98425	60	2.36220	320	12.59842		
26	1.02362	70	2.75590	330	12.99212		

1 mm = 0.03937 inch
1 cm = 0.3937 inch
1 m = 3.281 feet
1 inch = 25.4 mm
1 foot = 304.8 mm
1 yard = 914.4 mm

Imperial/Metric Conversion Chart

inch		mm	inch		mm	inch		mm
0	0	0	23/64	0.359375	9.1281	45/64	0.703125	17.8594
1/64	0.015625	0.3969				23/32	0.71875	18.2562
1/32	0.03125	0.7938	3/8	0.375	9.5250	47/64	0.734375	18.6531
3/64	0.046875	1.1906	25/64	0.390625	9.9219			
1/16	0.0625	1.5875	13/32	0.40625	10.3188	3/4	0.750	19.0500
			27/64	0.421875	10.7156			
5/64	0.078125	1.9844				49/64	0.765625	19.4469
3/32	0.09375	2.3812	7/16	0.4375	11.1125	25/32	0.78125	19.8438
7/64	0.109375	2.7781	29/64	0.453125	11.5094	51/64	0.796875	20.2406
			15/32	0.46875	11.9062	13/16	0.8125	20.6375
1/8	0.125	3.1750	31/64	0.484375	12.3031			
9/64	0.140625	3.5719				53/64	0.828125	21.0344
5/32	0.15625	3.9688	1/2	0.500	12.700	27/32	0.84375	21.4312
11/64	0.171875	4.3656	33/64	0.515625	13.0969	55/64	0.858375	21.8281
			17/32	0.53125	13.4938			
3/16	0.1875	4.7625	35/64	0.546875	13.8906	7/8	0.875	22.2250
13/64	0.203125	5.1594	9/16	0.5625	14.2875	57/64	0.890625	22.6219
7/32	0.21875	5.5562				29/32	0.90625	23.0188
15/64	0.234375	5.9531	37/64	0.578125	14.6844	59/64	0.921875	23.4156
1/4	0.250	6.3500	19/32	0.59375	15.0812			
			39/64	0.609375	15.4781	15/16	0.9375	23.8125
17/64	0.265625	6.7469				61/64	0.953125	24.2094
9/32	0.28125	7.1438	5/8	0.625	15.8750	31/32	0.96875	24.6062
19/64	0.296875	7.5406	41/64	0.640625	16.2719	63/64	0.984375	25.0031
5/16	0.3125	7.9375	21/32	0.65625	16.6688			
			43/64	0.671875	17.0656			
21/64	0.1328125	8.3344						
11/32	0.34375	8.7312	11/16	0.6875	17.4625	1 inch = 1.000 = 25.40 mm		

Index

TITLES AVAILABLE FROM
GMC Publications
BOOKS

<table>
<tr><td colspan="2">

WOODCARVING

The Art of the Woodcarver	GMC Publications
Carving Architectural Detail in Wood: The Classical Tradition	
	Frederick Wilbur
Carving Birds & Beasts	GMC Publications
Carving Nature: Wildlife Studies in Wood	Frank Fox-Wilson
Carving Realistic Birds	David Tippey
Decorative Woodcarving	Jeremy Williams
Elements of Woodcarving	Chris Pye
Essential Tips for Woodcarvers	GMC Publications
Essential Woodcarving Techniques	Dick Onians
Further Useful Tips for Woodcarvers	GMC Publications
Lettercarving in Wood: A Practical Course	Chris Pye
Making & Using Working Drawings for Realistic Model Animals	
	Basil F. Fordham
Power Tools for Woodcarving	David Tippey
Practical Tips for Turners & Carvers	GMC Publications
Relief Carving in Wood: A Practical Introduction	Chris Pye
Understanding Woodcarving	GMC Publications
Understanding Woodcarving in the Round	GMC Publications
Useful Techniques for Woodcarvers	GMC Publications
Wildfowl Carving – Volume 1	Jim Pearce
Wildfowl Carving – Volume 2	Jim Pearce
Woodcarving: A Complete Course	Ron Butterfield
Woodcarving: A Foundation Course	Zoë Gertner
Woodcarving for Beginners	GMC Publications
Woodcarving Tools & Equipment Test Reports	GMC Publications
Woodcarving Tools, Materials & Equipment	Chris Pye

WOODTURNING

Adventures in Woodturning	David Springett
Bert Marsh: Woodturner	Bert Marsh
Bowl Turning Techniques Masterclass	Tony Boase
Colouring Techniques for Woodturners	Jan Sanders
The Craftsman Woodturner	Peter Child
Decorative Techniques for Woodturners	Hilary Bowen
Fun at the Lathe	R.C. Bell
Further Useful Tips for Woodturners	GMC Publications
Illustrated Woodturning Techniques	John Hunnex
Intermediate Woodturning Projects	GMC Publications
Keith Rowley's Woodturning Projects	Keith Rowley
Practical Tips for Turners & Carvers	GMC Publications
Turning Green Wood	Michael O'Donnell
Turning Miniatures in Wood	John Sainsbury
Turning Pens and Pencils	Kip Christensen & Rex Burningham
Understanding Woodturning	Ann & Bob Phillips
Useful Techniques for Woodturners	GMC Publications
Useful Woodturning Projects	GMC Publications
Woodturning: Bowls, Platters, Hollow Forms, Vases, Vessels, Bottles, Flasks, Tankards, Plates	GMC Publications
Woodturning: A Foundation Course (New Edition)	Keith Rowley
Woodturning: A Fresh Approach	Robert Chapman
Woodturning: An Individual Approach	Dave Regester
Woodturning: A Source Book of Shapes	John Hunnex
Woodturning Jewellery	Hilary Bowen
Woodturning Masterclass	Tony Boase
Woodturning Techniques	GMC Publications
Woodturning Tools & Equipment Test Reports	GMC Publications
Woodturning Wizardry	David Springett

</td><td colspan="2">

WOODWORKING

Bird Boxes and Feeders for the Garden	Dave Mackenzie
Complete Woodfinishing	Ian Hosker
David Charlesworth's Furniture-Making Techniques	
	David Charlesworth
Furniture & Cabinetmaking Projects	GMC Publications
Furniture-Making Projects for the Wood Craftsman	GMC Publications
Furniture-Making Techniques for the Wood Craftsman	GMC Publications
Furniture Projects	Rod Wales
Furniture Restoration (Practical Crafts)	Kevin Jan Bonner
Furniture Restoration and Repair for Beginners	Kevin Jan Bonner
Furniture Restoration Workshop	Kevin Jan Bonner
Green Woodwork	Mike Abbott
Kevin Ley's Furniture Projects	Kevin Ley
Making & Modifying Woodworking Tools	Jim Kingshott
Making Chairs and Tables	GMC Publications
Making Classic English Furniture	Paul Richardson
Making Little Boxes from Wood	John Bennett
Making Shaker Furniture	Barry Jackson
Making Woodwork Aids and Devices	Robert Wearing
Minidrill: Fifteen Projects	John Everett
Pine Furniture Projects for the Home	Dave Mackenzie
Router Magic: Jigs, Fixtures and Tricks to Unleash your Router's Full Potential	Bill Hylton
Routing for Beginners	Anthony Bailey
Scrollsaw Pattern Book	John Everett
Scrollsaw Projects	GMC Publications
The Scrollsaw: Twenty Projects	John Everett
Sharpening: The Complete Guide	Jim Kingshott
Sharpening Pocket Reference Book	Jim Kingshott
Space-Saving Furniture Projects	Dave Mackenzie
Stickmaking: A Complete Course	Andrew Jones & Clive George
Stickmaking Handbook	Andrew Jones & Clive George
Test Reports: *The Router* and *Furniture & Cabinetmaking*	
	GMC Publications
Veneering: A Complete Course	Ian Hosker
Woodfinishing Handbook (Practical Crafts)	Ian Hosker
Woodworking with the Router: Professional Router Techniques any Woodworker can Use	
	Bill Hylton & Fred Matlack
The Workshop	Jim Kingshott

UPHOLSTERY

The Upholsterer's Pocket Reference Book	David James
Upholstery: A Complete Course (Revised Edition)	David James
Upholstery Restoration	David James
Upholstery Techniques & Projects	David James
Upholstery Tips and Hints	David James

TOYMAKING

Designing & Making Wooden Toys	Terry Kelly
Fun to Make Wooden Toys & Games	Jeff & Jennie Loader
Restoring Rocking Horses	Clive Green & Anthony Dew
Scrollsaw Toy Projects	Ivor Carlyle
Scrollsaw Toys for All Ages	Ivor Carlyle
Wooden Toy Projects	GMC Publications

</td></tr>
</table>

DOLLS' HOUSES AND MINIATURES

Architecture for Dolls' Houses	Joyce Percival
A Beginners' Guide to the Dolls' House Hobby	Jean Nisbett
The Complete Dolls' House Book	Jean Nisbett
The Dolls' House 1/24 Scale: A Complete Introduction	Jean Nisbett
Dolls' House Accessories, Fixtures and Fittings	Andrea Barham
Dolls' House Bathrooms: Lots of Little Loos	Patricia King
Dolls' House Fireplaces and Stoves	Patricia King
Easy to Make Dolls' House Accessories	Andrea Barham
Heraldic Miniature Knights	Peter Greenhill
Make Your Own Dolls' House Furniture	Maurice Harper
Making Dolls' House Furniture	Patricia King
Making Georgian Dolls' Houses	Derek Rowbottom
Making Miniature Gardens	Freida Gray
Making Miniature Oriental Rugs & Carpets	Meik & Ian McNaughton
Making Period Dolls' House Accessories	Andrea Barham
Making 1/12 Scale Character Figures	James Carrington
Making Tudor Dolls' Houses	Derek Rowbottom
Making Victorian Dolls' House Furniture	Patricia King
Miniature Bobbin Lace	Roz Snowden
Miniature Embroidery for the Georgian Dolls' House	Pamela Warner
Miniature Embroidery for the Victorian Dolls' House	Pamela Warner
Miniature Needlepoint Carpets	Janet Granger
More Miniature Oriental Rugs & Carpets	Meik & Ian McNaughton
Needlepoint 1/12 Scale: Design Collections for the Dolls' House	
	Felicity Price
The Secrets of the Dolls' House Makers	Jean Nisbett

CRAFTS

American Patchwork Designs in Needlepoint	Melanie Tacon
A Beginners' Guide to Rubber Stamping	Brenda Hunt
Blackwork: A New Approach	Brenda Day
Celtic Cross Stitch Designs	Carol Phillipson
Celtic Knotwork Designs	Sheila Sturrock
Celtic Knotwork Handbook	Sheila Sturrock
Celtic Spirals and Other Designs	Sheila Sturrock
Collage from Seeds, Leaves and Flowers	Joan Carver
Complete Pyrography	Stephen Poole
Contemporary Smocking	Dorothea Hall
Creating Colour with Dylon	Dylon International
Creative Doughcraft	Patricia Hughes
Creative Embroidery Techniques Using Colour Through Gold	
	Daphne J. Ashby & Jackie Woolsey
The Creative Quilter: Techniques and Projects	Pauline Brown
Decorative Beaded Purses	Enid Taylor
Designing and Making Cards	Glennis Gilruth
Glass Engraving Pattern Book	John Everett
Glass Painting	Emma Sedman
How to Arrange Flowers: A Japanese Approach to English Design	
	Taeko Marvelly
An Introduction to Crewel Embroidery	Mave Glenny
Making and Using Working Drawings for Realistic Model Animals	
	Basil F. Fordham
Making Character Bears	Valerie Tyler
Making Decorative Screens	Amanda Howes
Making Fairies and Fantastical Creatures	Julie Sharp
Making Greetings Cards for Beginners	Pat Sutherland
Making Hand-Sewn Boxes: Techniques and Projects	Jackie Woolsey
Making Knitwear Fit	Pat Ashforth & Steve Plummer
Making Mini Cards, Gift Tags & Invitations	Glennis Gilruth
Making Soft-Bodied Dough Characters	Patricia Hughes
Natural Ideas for Christmas: Fantastic Decorations to Make	
	Josie Cameron-Ashcroft & Carol Cox
Needlepoint: A Foundation Course	Sandra Hardy
Patchwork for Beginners	Pauline Brown
Pyrography Designs	Norma Gregory
Pyrography Handbook (Practical Crafts)	Stephen Poole
Ribbons and Roses	Lee Lockheed

Rose Windows for Quilters	Angela Besley
Rubber Stamping with Other Crafts	Lynne Garner
Sponge Painting	Ann Rooney
Tassel Making for Beginners	Enid Taylor
Tatting Collage	Lindsay Rogers
Temari: A Traditional Japanese Embroidery Technique	Margaret Ludlow
Theatre Models in Paper and Card	Robert Burgess
Wool Embroidery and Design	Lee Lockheed

VIDEOS

Drop-in and Pinstuffed Seats	David James
Stuffover Upholstery	David James
Elliptical Turning	David Springett
Woodturning Wizardry	David Springett
Turning Between Centres: The Basics	Dennis White
Turning Bowls	Dennis White
Boxes, Goblets and Screw Threads	Dennis White
Novelties and Projects	Dennis White
Classic Profiles	Dennis White
Twists and Advanced Turning	Dennis White
Sharpening the Professional Way	Jim Kingshott
Sharpening Turning & Carving Tools	Jim Kingshott
Bowl Turning	John Jordan
Hollow Turning	John Jordan
Woodturning: A Foundation Course	Keith Rowley
Carving a Figure: The Female Form	Ray Gonzalez
The Router: A Beginner's Guide	Alan Goodsell
The Scroll Saw: A Beginner's Guide	John Burke

MAGAZINES

WOODTURNING ◆ WOODCARVING

FURNITURE & CABINETMAKING

THE ROUTER ◆ WOODWORKING

THE DOLLS' HOUSE MAGAZINE

WATER GARDENING

EXOTIC GARDENING

GARDEN CALENDAR

OUTDOOR PHOTOGRAPHY

BUSINESSMATTERS

The above represents a full list of all titles currently published or scheduled to be published. All are available direct from the Publishers or through bookshops, newsagents and specialist retailers.
To place an order, or to obtain a complete catalogue, contact:

**GMC Publications,
Castle Place, 166 High Street, Lewes, East Sussex BN7 1XU, United Kingdom
Tel: 01273 488005 Fax: 01273 478606
E-mail: pubs@thegmcgroup.com**

Orders by credit card are accepted